Make Your Ow...
Silver
Jewellery

USING EVERYDAY TOOLS AND EASY TO OBTAIN MATERIALS

Acknowledgements

First and foremost, thank you to my beloved family for their love, help and support, and to my talented friends for the inspiration.

❧

Thanks also to my students who encouraged me to write a book, and to Pen and Sword Books Ltd for the opportunity to do so.

Mónica Weber-Butler

Make Your Own Silver Jewellery

USING EVERYDAY TOOLS AND EASY TO OBTAIN MATERIALS

Monica Weber-Butler

WHITE OWL

AN IMPRINT OF PEN & SWORD BOOKS LTD.
YORKSHIRE – PHILADELPHIA

First published in Great Britain in 2021 by
Pen & Sword WHITE OWL
An imprint of
Pen & Sword Books Ltd
Yorkshire – Philadelphia

ISBN 9781526780560

A CIP catalogue record for this book is
available from the British Library.

Printed and bound in India by Replika Press Pvt. Ltd.
Design: Paul Wilkinson

Pen & Sword Books Limited incorporates the imprints of Atlas, Archaeology, Aviation, Discovery, Family History, Fiction, History, Maritime, Military, Military Classics, Politics, Select, Transport, True Crime, Air World, Frontline Publishing, Leo Cooper, Remember When, Seaforth Publishing, The Praetorian Press, Wharncliffe Local History, Wharncliffe Transport, Wharncliffe True Crime and White Owl.

For a complete list of Pen & Sword titles please contact:
PEN & SWORD BOOKS LIMITED
47 Church Street, Barnsley, South Yorkshire, S70 2AS, England
E-mail: enquiries@pen-and-sword.co.uk
Website: www.pen-and-sword.co.uk

Or
PEN AND SWORD BOOKS
1950 Lawrence Rd, Havertown, PA 19083, USA
E-mail: Uspen-and-sword@casematepublishers.com
Website: www.penandswordbooks.com

Contents

Introduction

JEWELLERY-MAKING IS as old as time. Throughout history, our desire for adornment has motivated us to explore materials, and to develop tools, techniques and designs in order to create enduring beautiful objects. But jewellery is also used to express our individualism, particularly in an era of mass production.

In the 1990s, Mitsubishi Materials, a Japanese company, developed Precious Metal Clay (PMC), a clay-like material made of pulverised pure silver particles suspended in an organic binder, thus making the silver malleable and accessible to all. Once the clay has dried and is exposed to high temperatures (from a torch or a kiln), the binder burns off completely and the silver particles fuse together (sinter), leaving a solid, pure silver piece. Creating jewellery with silver metal clay requires some technical know-how, finesse and a little patience!

In this book you will learn how to create silver jewellery using simple everyday tools and easy to obtain materials. You will learn some basic silversmithing techniques, and explore the amazing possibilities that silver metal clay has to offer, using easy to follow instructions and step-by-step photos. You will also learn about the tools and materials needed, the safety aspects to be considered, and different design options.

The featured projects start with simple single pieces, ideal for earrings and charms, and progress all the way to a combination design for a statement pendant. Each project covers a different technique, builds upon your newly acquired skills and includes design options for greater individuality.

The inspirational gallery showcases projects that involve more advanced techniques, so you can see the possibilities silver metal clay has to offer. A list of resources and suppliers is also provided so that you can get started.

Since the introduction of silver metal clay, making jewellery has never been easier!

CHAPTER ONE

Safety

JEWELLERY-MAKING IS rewarding and engaging in equal measure, but if you only remember one thing about this book, let it be the Safety section.

Protect your eyes: always wear protective goggles. They are inexpensive, adjustable and light, so there's no excuse. Remember, wire brushes shed tiny pieces of metal as you scrub, and metal clay is made of tiny precious metal particles which could easily go into your eyes. Trust me, you don't want to play 'etch & sketch' with your vision.

Protect your nose: clay dust, metal particles and fumes are best avoided. Always work in a well-ventilated area, particularly when using patinas, firing metal clay or refilling a blowtorch. When refining the clay, do not create dust clouds. Instead of vigorous filing, gently run the file in one direction, or use the cosmetic sponge/wet wipe method.

Protect your hands: a drop of olive oil, or a touch of Badger Balm, moisturises your skin and creates a protective barrier between the palm of your hands and the clay (although the clay is non-toxic, prolonged use can dry the skin a little). Wear gloves when using patinas like Liver of Sulphur (LOS) or oxidising solutions, and protect the surface you are working on (a designated baking tray works well for this). Wash your hands as soon as you step away from your workbench and before you touch anything. Remember, tiny metal particles can cause major irritation in any tender parts of the body.

Be heat smart: never forget you are working with very hot pieces! Silver sinters at 900°C/1650°F. Always protect your eyes and tie back your hair. Avoid loose clothing (and avoid synthetic fabrics) and open-toed sandals when using a blowtorch. Wear a heavy-duty apron to protect your clothes: cotton or denim are ideal.

Protect the surface you are working on. Remove any flammable materials from your working area, and have a small fire extinguisher to hand if possible (you can get this at the supermarket), or some water.

Always place the blowtorch in front of you, as far away as possible. The blowtorch's nozzle remains hot for a long time. Always ignite the blowtorch away from you (if there is a gas leak due to a broken seal, the gas could ignite). Do not over tighten the knob of your blowtorch when you turn it off. Stop turning as soon as the hissing stops, otherwise you could damage the seal. Never try to refill a hot blowtorch.

Never touch a piece of metal or the firebrick after firing. They might not look hot, but they are! Remember, when cooling down the metal pieces (quenching), always touch the water first. If the water is cold, the piece will be cold; if the water is warm or hot, do not touch the piece.

Protect the environment: always follow the manufacturer's instructions to the letter! Always neutralise patinas with bicarbonate (unless not recommended by manufacturers) and tap water. Dispose of chemicals responsibly.

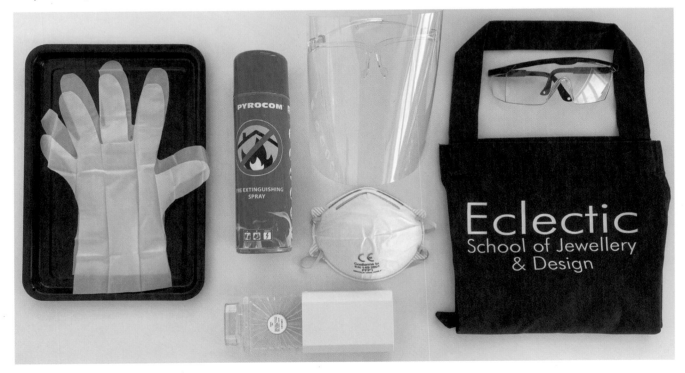

CHAPTER TWO

Materials

UNDERSTANDING SILVER: FINE VS STERLING.

Silver is a precious metal. We are all familiar with sterling silver, known as .925, but we are a little less familiar with fine silver. Fine silver is 99.9 per cent pure, whilst sterling silver is an alloy of fine silver and copper (or another base metal, like nickel). .925 refers to the percentage of silver and copper present: 92.5 per cent fine silver, and 7.5 per cent copper. Fine silver is a slightly softer metal. Sterling silver gets its strength from the alloy metal, and is more durable, hence its popularity and extensive use. The downside is that some people are allergic to the alloy metals mixed with the silver, and thus shy away from wearing silver jewellery.

SILVER METAL CLAY

Silver metal clay is a malleable material made of pulverised fine silver particles suspended in an organic binder, which can be easily shaped, textured and cut. Once the water in the binder has completely evaporated, the dry clay is exposed to a high temperature from a torch (or a kiln). As the binder burns off completely, the silver particles fuse together (sinter), leaving a solid, fine silver piece. Note that the packet displays two weights. The large print number indicates the amount of silver; the small number below is the weight of the silver and binder combined.

There are several fine silver metal clay brands on the market: PMC (Plus, Flex, PMC3), Art Clay, Aussie Metal Clay, FS999, etc. PMC3, Flex and Art Clay can be torch fired with good results (follow manufacturers' firing schedules). I work mainly with PMC3, and use both a blowtorch for small light pieces, and a kiln for large and three-dimensional (3D) pieces. For the projects in this book a butane blowtorch works well.

Shrinkage:

Metal clay shrinks from all directions (length, width, thickness), pulling itself from the centre (you can see this happen as you fire it). The binder's burn-off results in a slight shrinkage of the pieces (8 to 15 per cent, depending on the brand and type of clay). The shrinkage sharpens texture definition and so is not a bad thing.

Flat pieces are the easiest to fire because the metal is supported throughout. You will be able to see the piece curl up from the edges, and then go flat again.

Occasionally, a piece might curve up (or down), and need a little help to go back to shape. This is caused by 'surface drag', which happens when the silver begins to shrink but is hampered by the surface of the firebrick it is sitting on during firing. Sometimes the curvature is pleasing, but for those occasions when it isn't, a little gentle tapping with a nylon mallet restores the piece to its original flat state.

Sintering: Time, Temperature and Strength

The melting point of fine silver is 961°C/1763°F. Fine silver clay is just below its melting point at sintering temperatures during the firing process, at 900°C/1650°F. The longer the fine silver clay is held at its sintering temperature, the stronger the bond individual particles form with each other.

Adjust firing times according to the size and thickness of your pieces: two minutes for a small thin piece (2cm diameter), three minutes for a medium piece (3cm diameter), and five minutes for a large piece (4–5cm diameter). As a rule of thumb, add an extra minute for each centimetre in diameter (start the minute count from the moment the metal reaches a pale salmon colour), and preferably use a larger torch for larger pieces.

MOULDING MATERIALS

Two part moulding compound is a putty-like material that sets once the two parts are combined. It is used to create flexible moulds of textures, plants and objects.

FINDINGS GUIDE

Findings are the components used in jewellery-making, such as earring hooks, connectors, clasps and fasteners, chains, wire, stringing materials, beads, bails, etc. This guide should help you to select the correct item.

EARRING HOOKS

Fish hooks are the most commonly used earring findings. They are light, and easy to use and wear. They are also easy to make (see Versatile Rods chapter for instructions), or can be bought ready-made. There are many different styles of fish hooks, some plain,

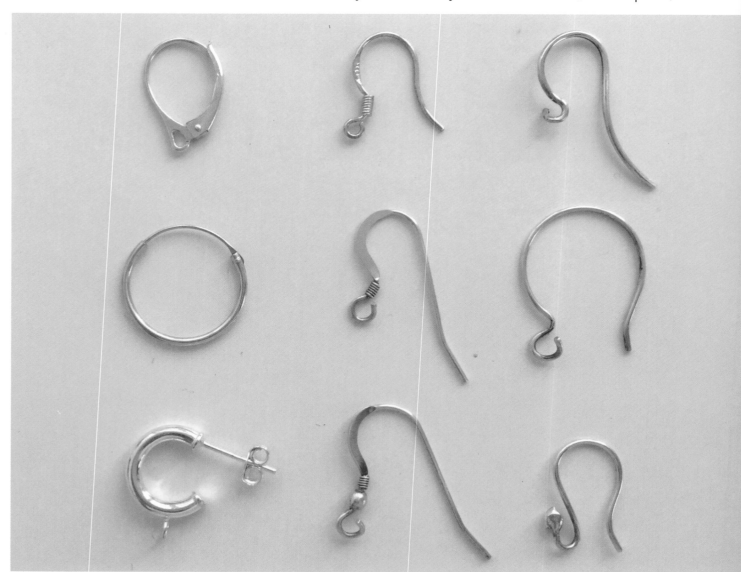

small and a little flimsy, and others long, ornate and made with a heavier-gauge wire. The downside of fish hooks is that they can easily be lost.

Kidney wires are similar in appearance to fish hooks, but kidney wires have a hook fastener at the back, which makes them more secure. They are a little more complicated to make, so many people prefer to buy them ready-made.

Leverback hooks are a step above! Leverback hooks look more professional; they are secure and easy to wear. However, they might require an additional jump ring to enable a design element to hang facing forward.

Ear post/studs with ring. These earring findings offer a different look. The most common posts have a ball as the main feature, but other options like small cubes, a single cubic zirconia (in assorted colours), or floral designs are available. The ring below the main feature is used to attach dangles and charms. The fasteners can be a little fiddly and easy to lose, so have some spare.

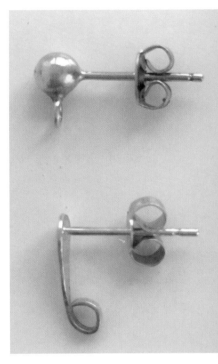

Hoops. Although earrings in their own right, they can be used to display decorative elements too. Hoops come in a number of styles, weights and sizes. They provide the option of having interchangeable decorative elements. They are safe and easy to wear.

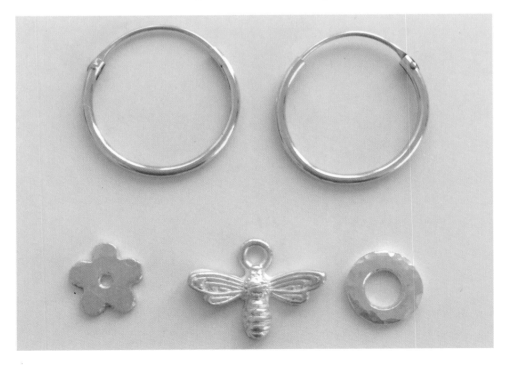

Three-quarter hoops are a great way to present your creations! They are made with curved hollowed tubes, making them light, and the post-fastening makes them almost impossible to lose! The hoop prettily embraces the earlobe, showcasing decorative elements and providing free movement. A simple silver disc becomes an elegant fashion accessory when paired with three-quarter hoops.

Chandeliers are used to suspend multiple decorative elements. Chandeliers are ideal for more elaborate designs. Some include an ear hook, and some need to be attached to one. For the latter, ensure the ear hook complements the overall design.

Non-pierced ears clip-on. As the name suggests, these are ideal for those who do not have piercings. Decorative elements must be lightweight, otherwise they will dislodge the earring. If the spring on the clip-ons is too strong they can become uncomfortable to wear.

CONNECTORS

Connectors join different parts together, and fall into different categories. They can be headpins, eyepins, jump rings, links or spacer bars.

Some connectors are made of wire, and it is therefore important to understand a little about wire. The thickness of the wire is referred to as gauge. The higher the gauge number, the thinner the wire. When the measurements are in inches or millimetres the opposite is true: the higher the number the thicker the wire.

Headpins are used to attach beads or pearls to earring hooks, or pendants, either with a simple loop or with a wrapped loop (see Versatile Rods chapter). The head can have a flat end, a single ball end (in assorted sizes), a triple ball end or be spear ended. The gauge, ball size and lengths vary, so make sure you work out the correct size for your project. Allow ½ inch of free wire after beads to create a wrapped loop or ¼ inch to create a simple loop/eye with the round-nose pliers.

Eyepins, when combined with beads, pearls or silver pieces, are ideal for creating links and decorative elements. The gauge, eye size and length vary, so plan carefully for your project. Eyepins can also be used as fringes to add movement to a design. Allow ¼ inch

A selection of commercially available ready-made connectors.

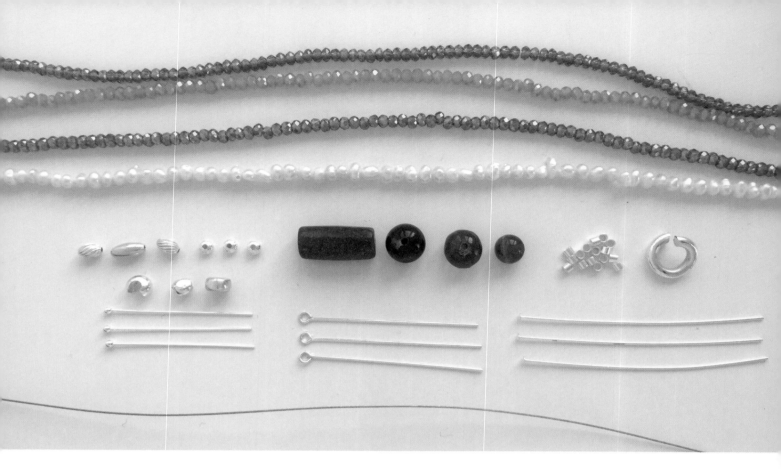

From the top: semi-precious faceted rondells, rice pearls, assorted silver beads, semi-precious beads, crimps, jump ring, ball pins, eye pins, head pins and stringing wire.

of free wire after beads to create a second eye/simple loop with the round-nose pliers.

Jump rings are an essential jewellery-making component! Jump rings are used to join different pieces together, as a bail, and can be used to create chainmail too. It is important to use the correct gauge for the job: a high gauge will lack strength, and a low-gauge jump ring could overpower a design.

Ready-made jump rings are sold as open or closed. Open jump rings are used to join elements together. Closed rings are soldered or fused, and are useful for stringing since this eliminates the risk of coming undone. Jump rings can easily be made (see Basic Techniques chapter). When opening a jump ring, push the sides past each other (north–south). This method enables you to reverse the process and preserves the circular form of the jump ring. Never open a jump ring by pulling the sides apart as this will distort the circle and weaken the ring.

Links are decorative pieces with a ring opening at both ends, thus enabling them to be attached to something else. Links can be the focal point of a chain, or bracelet. They can also be a decorative extension for an earring or pendant. There are many designs readily

available, or you can create your own for a bespoke look. Something as simple as a hammered disc (with openings at at opposite sides) attached to a chain can make a very pretty necklace.

Spacer bars are used to keep multiple strands of beads or pearls aligned. They can be very thin and discreet, or very prominent. Spacer bars start with two holes, and can have as many as ten. The visible edges can be plain or ornate. Making spacer bars with metal clay is simple and enables you to create bespoke jewellery pieces.

CLASPS AND FASTENERS

Clasps and fasteners hold a piece together, are part of the overall design and can also be the focal point. Choose wisely! An overpowering or unattractive clasp can significantly change the perception of a piece.

There are many different clasps and fasteners on the market, and some are easier to use than others. All clasps and fasteners can be found in different sizes, so you can seamlessly incorporate them into your designs. Remember that the vast majority of people are right handed, so the clasp must always be on the right-hand side of a chain or necklace, and the tab (or ring) on the left; this will facilitate use.

Spring-rings are the most common types of clasp. Sometimes spring-rings are sold as a set that includes a tab (or ring) for the

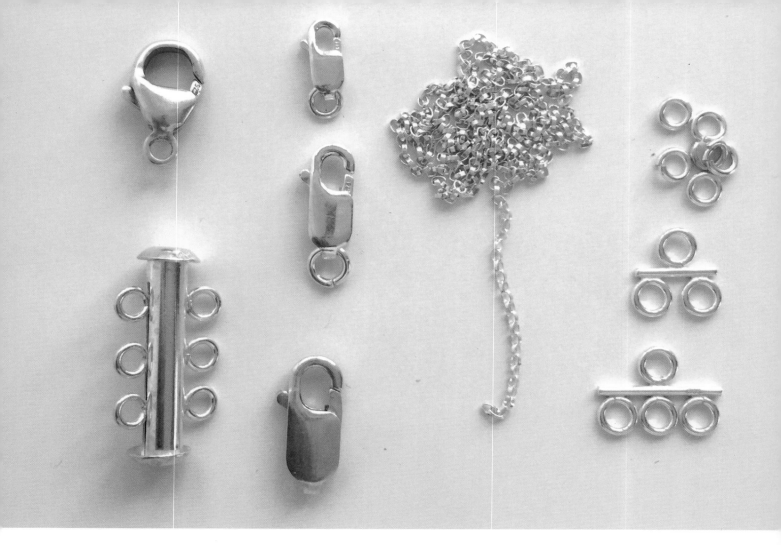

Clasps, loose chain, jump rings and connectors (one to two, and one to three rings).

other end of the chain or necklace. When they are sold on their own, use a jump ring to close (make sure the jump ring fits through the opening on the side of the spring-ring). The downside of a spring-ring is that the opening can be small and the lever can be tiny, making it difficult to use.

Lobster clasps are my personal favourite. They sit flat on the neck and have a bigger opening, making them easy to use. Some lobster clasps have a decorative design, like a heart shape, or are shaped like a teardrop.

Barrel clasps screw closed and look like a bicone bead, so they are discreet, but can be a little fiddly to close.

Magnetic clasps are easy to use, but can be very unattractive on their own! This means they require a casing or well-positioned bead caps (or cones) to house them.

Toggles are sold as a two-part set: a ring and a bar that feeds through the ring. Toggles come in many shapes and sizes. They can be incorporated into the design or be the focal point.

S-Hooks are a very simple closure design. You can see them in museum collections of early jewellery pieces. They are effective, but care must be taken to keep the loops tight, so they do not come undone with use. Some modern versions have one side of the 'S' soldered closed, making them safer to wear. S-hooks are sold with two jump rings (one on each end) or without them so, if not supplied, make sure you choose a closed, low-gauge jump ring that will withstand use.

Chain extensions are used to elongate a chain or necklace, thus providing a variety of lengths for a single jewellery piece.

STRINGING MATERIALS

If you are planning to use beaded elements in your designs, you will need a way of keeping the beads together. Whether you are making necklaces or bracelets to showcase your silver creations, these stringing materials will open up a world of possibilities.

Beading thread comes in a variety of materials, such as polyester, nylon, cotton, silk and blends. Beading thread is suitable for lightweight designs or woven/knotted projects. It is advisable to coat fine beading thread with beeswax to make it easier to use, and to hide the knots inside suitable ending findings.

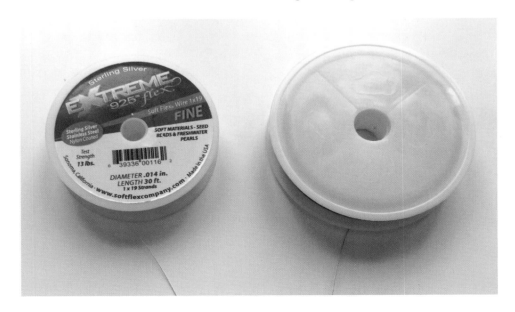

Beading wire: Sterling silver (left), Tiger tail (right).

Beading wire (Tiger tail) is made up of multiple coated strands of wire (stainless steel, or silver), making it strong and durable. Beading wire is suitable for heavy beads and pendants. Crimps are used to secure this beading wire.

Loose chain is sold in metric lengths, and in a variety of styles. Select loose chain that has open links: oval link, round rolo, long rolo, open curb or flat oval. The chain description often tells you the correct jump ring size the chain will accept.

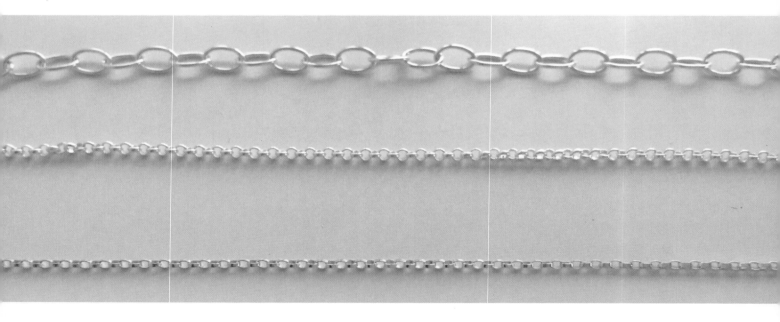

Monofilament is a clear fishing cord used when the design requires the cord to remain invisible through the beads. Crimps are used to secure this beading wire.

Hemp, Cotton, Leather, Suede and Silk cords and ribbons are generally used in projects with simple knotted designs, for a more rustic/organic look. These cords and ribbons might require ending findings, depending on the design.

Stretchy cord (Jelly cord) is great for beading bracelets and anklets without a clasp or fastener. A drop of superglue on the stretch knot is all that is needed to secure it.

Bead Stoppers prevent beads and components from slipping off the stringing material while you work.

Crimps are vital components in jewellery-making. Crimps are used with beading wire to secure a clasp, and can also be used as spacers and as beads. There are different sizes (from 1.5mm x 2mm to 2.5mm x 2.5mm), and materials (sterling, copper, brass, etc.) for all weights and styles of beading. Sterling silver tube crimps are the most common. End crimps have a ring on top so a clasp can be added. Use with crimp pliers, in the correct size, to ensure a neat and firm hold (see Tools section).

Superglue and two-part epoxy glue are used to secure knots, and to attach certain components made of different materials like sterling silver and leather or rubber (in jewellery-making this process is often referred to as 'chemical bonding'). Always protect your eyes, use in well-ventilated areas, and follow the manufacturer's instructions to the letter.

ENDINGS

Endings are essential parts of jewellery-making. They prettily house, or cover, unsightly but necessary elements, like large holes, knots, crimps, wires and loose ends. Bead-caps, cones, end-crimps, crimp-covers, leather-end fasteners and cord-ends fall into this category.

Cones are used to house knots, and for connecting the ends of multi-strand projects.

End crimps are ideal for leather, ribbon, cord or hemp. Fold over the ends with a drop of superglue to hold the cord in place.

Cord-ends come in assorted gauges for use with leather thongs and cords. Cord ends cover a wide range, from crimpable to glue-in ends; some designs also incorporate a clasp. In order to get the correct size refer to the cord-end ID (inner diameter) and match it to the leather cord thickness.

Bead caps enable you to cover up the large holes some beads have

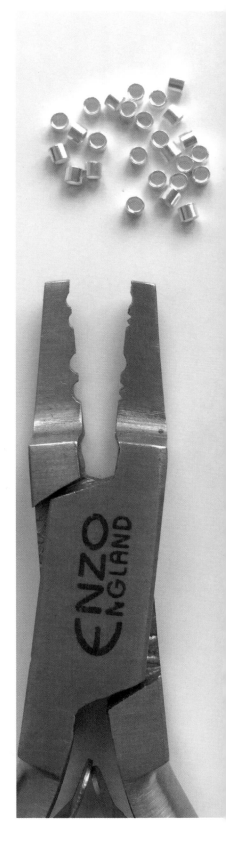

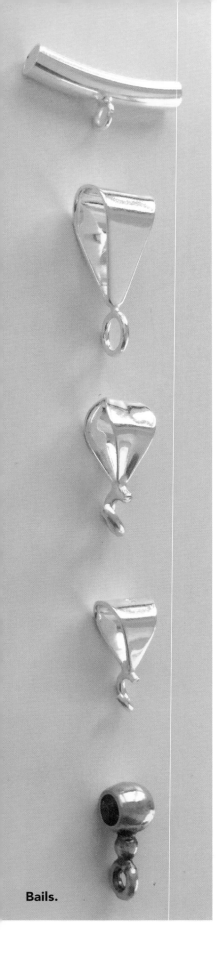

Bails.

(like handmade glass beads), or transition from an arrangement of beads into a new section of a piece.

BEADS

There is a huge range of beads on the market! Styles, shapes, sizes, colours and materials vary greatly too. From pearls, glass and semi-precious stones to base and precious metals. (I work mainly with sterling silver, pearls, Swarovski crystals and semi-precious stones.) You can mix and match, but ensure your selection works well together and does not damage other components or the stringing materials. It is advisable to have a size chart next to you when ordering online to avoid costly mistakes.

Bead board and mats are useful (but not essential) when working out the layout of a bead pattern, since they keep the components in place. Bead boards have multiple length grooves and useful wells where beads and components can be safely stored. Bead mats are 'fuzzy' and flexible, so can be rolled up and easily stored. It is advisable to have a non-slip surface to work on, to prevent beads going everywhere (even a small towel will do).

BAILS

Bails are findings that allow a chain or stringing material to pass through. They are connected to a ring, and used to attach a bead, or silver piece. They can have a single ring or have multiple ones. A bail is normally placed in the centre of a necklace or chain. Bails come in different styles and sizes, so choose one that complements your design.

Assorted sterling
sliver beads strung
with sterling silver
wire to create a
bespoke necklace.

CHAPTER THREE

Tools

METAL CLAY TOOLS AND EQUIPMENT

A little history

When silver metal clay was first introduced in the 1990s, the manufacturers had this brilliant material, but no specific tools to work with it. They therefore approached a group of talented artists from different disciplines for advice, and they came up with some suggestions to make the material accessible to all. A consistent terminology was agreed upon, so everyone could follow the instructions and have positive results.

The number of metal clay and jewellery-making tools and gadgets available on the market is mind boggling! But in reality you need only a few basic items to work with metal clay (which you can either buy, make or find around the house). The tools fall into three categories: forming, drying and refining, and firing and finishing. You will also need a few traditional silversmithing tools to successfully complete the projects in this book.

FORMING TOOLS

Depth/thickness slats or cards. These are used to produce a consistent thickness when working with metal clay. The same number of depth cards are placed at either side of the clay, so that a roller can be used to produce an even 'sheet' of clay. The minimum thickness for a piece is three cards or 0.75mm.

All the projects include a thickness guide expressed in 'cards'. The reason for this goes back to the group of artists, who used playing cards to obtain consistent results. Nowadays it is possible to buy sets of colour-coded depth/thickness slats which match different card thicknesses, but you can also make your own with a set of large plastic-coated playing cards and some superglue (instructions on the following page).

Slat colour		Inches	mm	Cards
		0.01	0.25	1
		0.02	0.50	2
		0.03	0.75	3
		0.04	1.00	4
		0.06	1.50	6
		0.08	2.00	8

Please note that the slat colours vary from supplier to supplier, but the corresponding thicknesses should be the same.

HOW TO MAKE YOUR OWN DEPTH/THICKNESS CARDS

You will need:
- A pack of plastic-coated Jumbo playing cards (85mm x 125mm). **Do not use standard size cards**.
- Superglue.
- Scissors, or craft knife and cutting mat.
- Protective goggles.
- Protective surface.

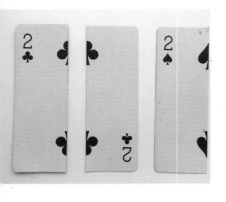

1. Select a card suit (e.g. ♠), and separate eight cards – ace to 8. Cut them in half lengthwise. Please note: it is important to cut the cards first, since the glue and increasing card thickness would make it difficult to do so afterwards.

2. Select a second suit, the same colour as the previous one (e.g. ♣) and separate cards 2 to 8 (you should have either red cards or black, as this will avoid confusion). Cut these in half lengthwise and set them aside. These two suits are your 'bookends', the cards you will still see when the slats cards are finished.

3. Select an additional twenty-one random cards. Cut in half lengthwise.

4. To assemble a two-depth/thickness card, apply a drop of glue to the reverse side of one half of the number 2 card from your first suit and attach to the back of it the corresponding number 2 half from your second suit. The cards should be back to back, so you are able to see the numbers on both sides at all times. Repeat with the other number 2 halves so that you have two finished slats, each of depth 2 cards.

5. To assemble a third depth/thickness card, apply a drop of glue to the reverse side of one half of the number 3 card from your first suit and attach to any half from the random cards. Then 'sandwich' the random card by attaching the back of the corresponding number 3 half from your second suit. Remember, the cards should be back to back, so you are able to see the same numbers on both sides.

6. Repeat the process with the rest of the cards, increasing the number of different colour cards to match the numbers, but including the 'bookend' in the count, so you should have:

1♠
2♠ + 2♣
3♠ + one random card + 3♣
4♠ + two random cards + 4♣
5♠ + three random cards + 5♣
6♠ + four random cards + 6♣
7♠ + five random cards + 7♣
8♠ + six random cards + 8♣

Remember to count all the cards before you glue them together.

Roller. This is just a length of PVC or acrylic tube around 16cm long and 2cm in diameter. It is used to evenly extend the clay using the depth cards. Each end of the roller rests on a depth-card and the clay sits between them.

Lubricants: Olive oil or Badger Balm (avoid mineral oils like baby oil, because they interfere with the binder in the clay). A drop of olive oil (or a touch of balm) is used as a barrier on the palm of the hands to prevent drying the clay, prolong its malleability and to stop it sticking to you. Rubbing the excess oil on the roller, the work surface and the edges of metal cutters is good practice.

Smooth work surface. This could be a single ceramic tile, a place mat, a granite or marble board, a piece of acrylic or Perspex, etc.

Project mats. These are placed over the work surface, and are used to roll out, texture and cut the clay. You could use the rest of the playing cards as project mats, or make your own with reusable Teflon sheet (used for baking) or flush folders/page protectors. Simply cut into medium size rectangles (85mm x 125mm). If you live in a warm climate, or work in a warm room, use page protectors cut widthways, so you can place the clay between the two halves to retain moisture (lubricate first with a little olive oil, or Badger Balm). Remember that the clay will pick up the texture of your project mat, so ensure it is as smooth as possible if you want a mirror finish, or that any pattern on it complements your designs.

Needle tool. This handy tool is used to cut, shape and lift the clay (it is the equivalent of a jeweller's saw). There are a few to choose from, but the best have a fine needle and a comfortable handle (they

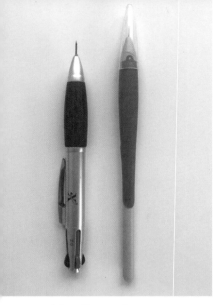

Needle tools.

were originally created for the parchment craft). Some needle tools come in a pen that also includes three different-sized embossing balls. Although the needle is a little thicker, they work well.

Geometric Templates/Stencils. These come in a variety of shapes and sizes. They are used in conjunction with the needle tool to cut out shapes.

Craft clay cutters and cake decorating cutters. There is a great variety of cutters available, in every shape you can imagine. Just remember that you are working on a small scale (some cutters can be huge!), and that you can use a stencil and needle tool instead.

Small paintbrush. Useful to smooth out blemishes, and apply water or metal clay paste.

Small spray bottle for water. Ideal for rehydrating or reconstituting the clay.

Scalpel or fine craft knife. Used to cut down or lift clay.

Tissue blade set of three (rigid, flexible and wavy). These are really useful for cutting straight edges, curves and waves. They are very sharp, so store in a designated container (like a travel toothbrush holder).

Toothbrush with cover. This has multiple uses, like spreading lubricant (olive oil or Badger Balm) on surfaces, stamps and texture plates (apply a drop of olive oil, or a little Badger Balm, to the bristles and rub the surface of the texture plate or stamp with it). It is also great for texturing clay, and it helps to dislodge bits of dried clay from cutters, etc. The cover keeps the dust and contaminants at bay.

Texture plates and stamps. Commercially available texture plates and stamps can be successfully used with metal clay. They are particularly good when creating multiple pieces, or consistent designs. It is a good idea to modify or personalise these types of texture, by adding decorative elements, removing sections, or mixing and matching. That way your jewellery will look different from the creations of other users of the same textures. Texture plates must be lubricated before use.

Transparent acrylic block for stamping (100mm x 130mm). These are often sold as sets, but you can also get them individually. Acrylic blocks are used with unmounted stamps. For metal clay they are used to exert even pressure on texture

Acrylic block.

plates. They are also used to roll out rods by rolling back and forth over a piece of clay, and as a firm base when making moulds.

DRYING AND REFINING

Metal clay can be allowed to dry naturally, but if you wish to speed up the process here are a few options:

An electric pancake maker is perfect for the job! It has a large surface, so it can accommodate multiple pieces, and it has a temperature control (the lowest setting is the best). The mini version comes with a cover too, which can help to prevent accidental contact with the warm surface.

Food dehydrators gently blow warm air from the base, so the drying process takes a little longer, but they come with multiple drying trays, making them great for mass production. The least expensive version of food dehydrator would do nicely.

Cup warmers are ideal for small spaces. The small disc area accommodates a few pieces at once, so you can work on multiple projects. Select one that can be used without connecting it to a computer.

Always use a spatula to remove the pieces from any of the above appliances. Remember, the clay is made of metal and will retain heat. Transfer the pieces from the heat source onto the steel block to absorb the heat first (it only takes a few seconds). Also, remember to disconnect the appliance when not in use.

Cling film is used with small tube cutters (ferrules) to create small decorative elements. Simply roll out a clay sheet, cover it with cling film, then use the cutter over the film. As the film stretches over the clay it rounds the edges of the divot. Allow to dry, then attach with a drop of water.

Nail files/emery boards/salon boards (fine, not coarse). These commonly used files work wonders on dry metal clay. Work in one direction and rotate your clay piece instead of going back and forth.

Cosmetic wedges are dampened in clean water, and then gently rubbed over rough edges to smooth them out.

Toothpicks (round) are ideal for cleaning small orifices. Simply place in the orifice and gently twirl (do not push!). They are also very useful to create textures on the clay.

Wire connectors (ferrules) are coloured-coded mini metal tubes in assorted sizes (from 0.5mm to 10mm). The soft metal the connectors are made from enables you to modify them with pliers (and a little patience), so you can customise them for your projects (see Lacuna chapter).

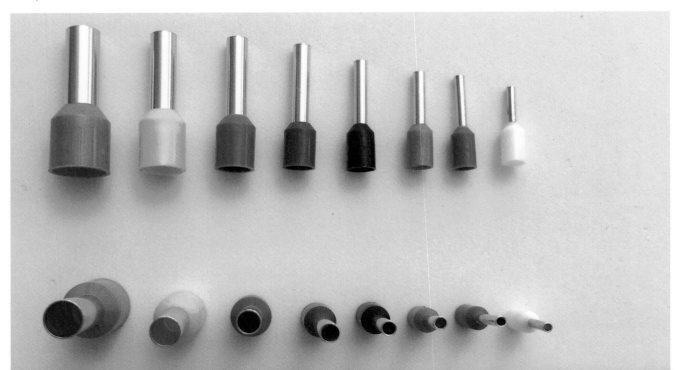

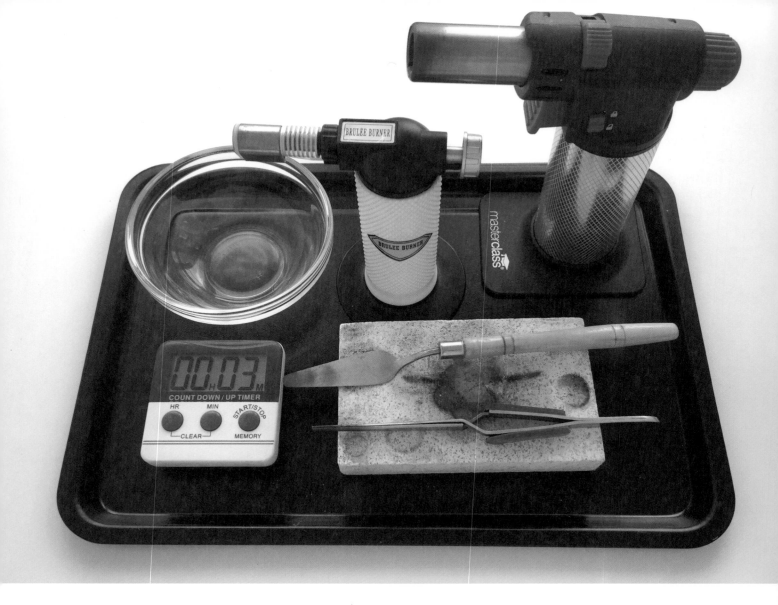

FIRING AND FINISHING

FIRING

Clear protective goggles are a MUST, so you can keep enjoying the beautiful sights of this world. Always protect your eyes.

Cotton canvas apron. Protects your clothing and is an extra layer between your skin and a hot piece of metal. It is important to wear natural fibres, rather than synthetic (which melt when exposed to heat).

Baking tray (plain, non-stick) keeps all your firing equipment together, protects your surfaces and contains any spills.

Firebrick/Soldering brick (230mm x 114mm x 25mm). This is where the magic happens!

Firebricks are made of heat-resistant materials like vermiculite. Always place the brick onto the baking tray before use.

Timer. Firing metal clay requires accurate timing. However, this does not mean you need to get something fancy! A digital kitchen timer which you can turn on/off with one hand would be perfect.

Insulated reverse action tweezers. Ideal for holding small parts and components in position hands-free, or to take the strain of constant squeezing.

Blowtorch (refillable). There are many types of blowtorch available. The best for metal clay projects are the ones used for cooking which use butane gas. These fall into three nozzle categories: small, medium and large. Small nozzles are good for soldering and precision work. Large nozzles generate more heat, which is good for sintering, but can be cumbersome and can easily melt a piece of silver. If you are only buying one, go for medium-sized nozzle, so you get the best of both worlds.

Artist spatula set (three or five). This inexpensive set of metal spatulas will make your life easier! They are great for moving hot pieces from the firebrick into the water dish, and also for placing/removing pieces on the hot plate of the drying equipment.

Small heat-resistant glass dish. It is important to use a dish that will not shatter with sudden temperature changes. These glass dishes can be found in the kitchen section of your local supermarket.

Small fire extinguisher. It is a good idea to have fire safety equipment as a precaution. I have been working with blowtorches since 2003, and am happy to say that my extinguisher has never been used.

FINISHING
Rubber or nylon block. A forgiving surface used as a support for wire-brushing the fired silver. The material gently 'grabs' the silver, but does not scratch it, as it is being brushed with a damp wire brush.

Brass or stainless steel wire brush. These are the first step in the

polishing process. The silver looks 'frosty' after being fired, because the surface of the metal has uneven planes at this stage (peaks and valleys). Brushing begins to even out the planes and the silver becomes more reflective. It is important to dip the wire bristles in a little water prior to brushing, to prevent particle transference (which makes the silver look yellowish).

Agate burnisher. The smooth agate surface glides over the silver, compressing it and bringing the metal to a lovely high sheen without leaving tool marks (but avoid using the tip of the tool or you will create grooves!). Treat your agate burnisher tenderly: do not drop it or it will break. Do not store with other tools or it will get chipped.

Cork mat and various blocks.

Polish and polishing cloths provide the finishing touches to your creations. A soft cloth (old T-shirts are ideal) and a little good quality silver polish (either cream, liquid or FFFF grade pumice powder) will bring out the shine. Keep all your polishing aids clean to avoid contamination from metal dust (which can cause scratches on the silver).

If you would like a little mechanical assistance, an inexpensive **mini drill (with bit set)**, or an **electric nail file**, will do the job (battery- or mains-operated); just make sure you use soft mop heads to buff the silver.

Safety first: remember to protect your eyes, tie back your hair and avoid loose clothing when using power tools.

SILVERSMITHING TOOLS

The following items are essential for jewellery-making in general. These tools last a lifetime so make sure you are happy with your

TIP: Many nail art tools and products are surprisingly useful for metal clay, and often are considerably less expensive than traditional jewellery-making tools.

choice. Do shop around before committing to buy, since prices can vary greatly (look for sets and bundle offers).

Safety first: Protective goggles, dust mask and plastic gloves. Always protect your eyes, nose, hands, and furnishings.

SHAPING, TEXTURING AND WORK HARDENING

Watchmaker's hammer used for 'line' texturing (narrow end), and work hardening small pieces (flat end).

1 inch chasing hammer/ ball pein planishing hammer for 'hammered finish' texturing (ball end) and work hardening (flat end).

Nylon hammer or rubber mallet used to gently reshape a piece without marking the metal.

Steel and rubber bench block (60mm x 60mm x 25mm, or 75mm diameter). Small anvil used to texture and shape metals. The bottom rubber base can be used to wire-brush fired silver (remove the steel block first to prevent rust). Please note that some models come with interchangeable blocks (steel and nylon blocks in a rubber base).

Cork mat (kitchen pot stand/coaster) protects your furniture when using the steel block. Even though the hammering involved in jewellery-making is gentle, always place the steel block on the cork mat, and make sure you work above the leg of your table (this provides extra support).

Tool care: take good care of your tools. Remember, any blemish on the hammer's head, or on the steel block, will transfer to the silver surface, so polish the heads and the surface of the block if necessary.

PLIERS

These are your forming tools. Make sure they are good quality, and that they sit comfortably in your hand.

Chain-nose pliers (also called long-nose pliers) have smooth tapered tips to reach into small places, and hold small delicate pieces without marking the metal.

Bent-nose pliers (non-serrated) are ideal for those hard-to-reach places. Used in conjunction with other pliers, they facilitate holding delicate pieces, opening and closing jump rings, and making small adjustments.

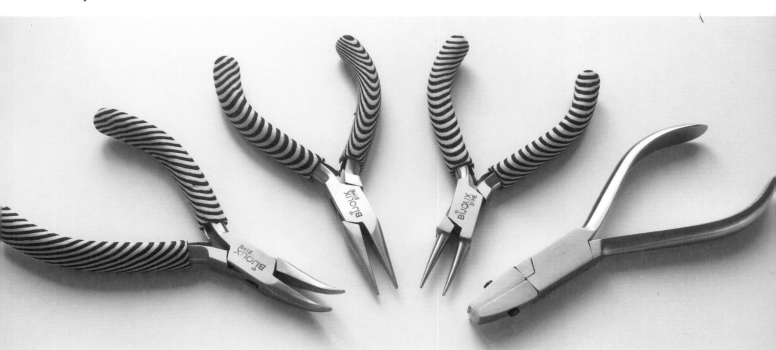

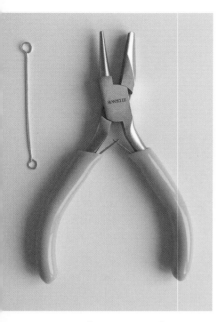

Round concave pliers.

Crimping pliers and how to use them (opposite page).

Round-nose pliers are used to create loops, coils and jump rings.

Round concave pliers are your friend! The concave lower jaw helps to easily form loops (both simple and wrapped), rings or curves in wire, headpins and eyepins.

Double nylon flat jaw pliers straighten wire as they glide over the surface.

Three-stepped forming pliers. Used to form multiple jump rings, or bails at once. The nose of this set of pliers has two different sides. One side of the nose is long, uniform and covered in plastic tubing to prevent marring the metal, the other side of the nose has three different diameter barrels. The wire is wrapped over the selected size.

Flush wire cutters (electrical cable cutters) are essential for cutting and trimming wire. The best ones, which have narrow triangular jaws, cut one side of the wire perfectly flat and leave only a small apex on the other side of the cut. Unfortunately, most jewellery-making tool kits include flush cutters with rounded jaws that leave an apex on both sides of the cut wire.

Bead-crimping pliers enable you to secure crimps to your stringing material. The most commonly available crimping pliers are used with 2mm x 2mm crimps (smaller crimps require mini crimping pliers), but it is possible to buy crimping pliers that have grooves for standard and mini crimps. The jaw has two grooves: the one closer to the handle (which has a notch) is used first to collapse

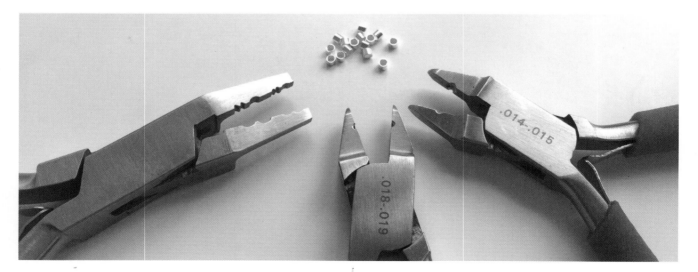

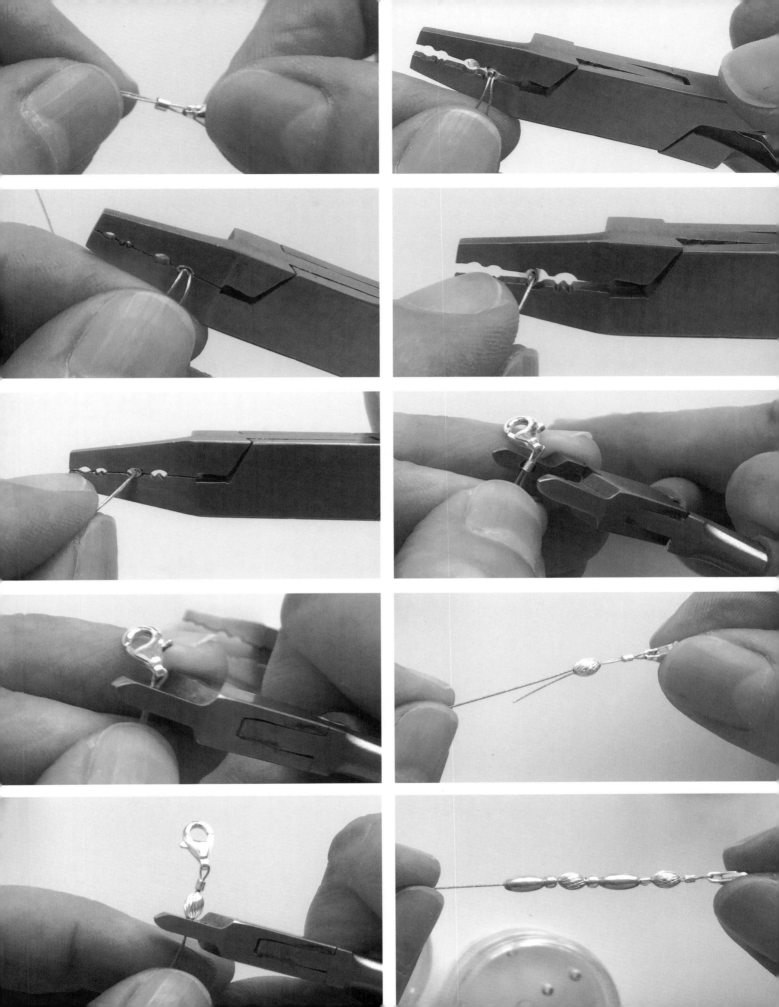

the crimp in the centre. The second groove compresses the crimp onto itself (you need to rotate the crimp 90 degrees to a vertical position). There are some crimping pliers (magic crimpers) that create a small 'sphere', which looks pretty but is not as secure, since they only pinch the top and bottom edge of the crimp instead of the full length of it. However, magic crimpers can be used to 'round' the edges of a compressed crimp.

OTHERS

Pin vice hand drill and mini bits set (also known as mini hand drill with keyless chuck) enables you to perforate pieces in both the clay and metal stage. It is also useful to enlarge existing holes.

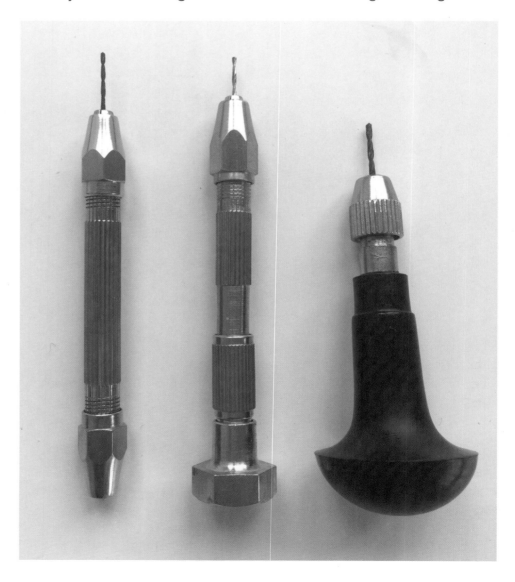

Mini diamond needle files (140mm x 3mm), or bead reamer set. These finishing tools are used to clean clogged holes in beads, refine/reshape rough edges or enlarge openings.

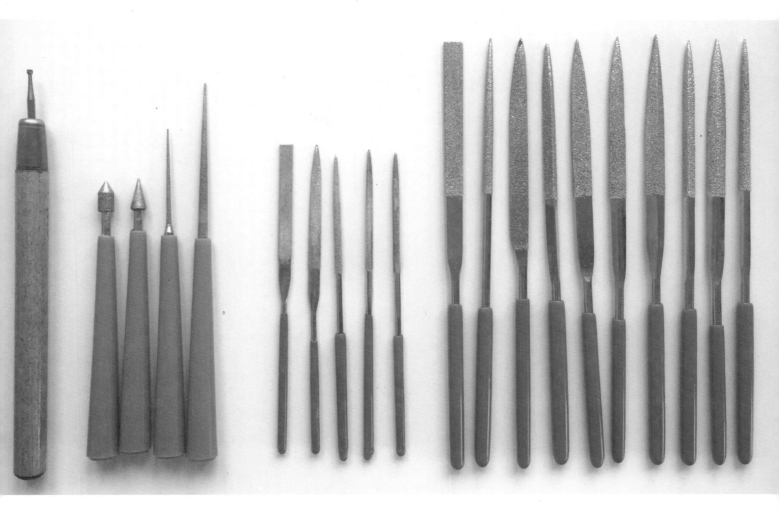

Wire rounder tool for jewellery-making. Used for rounding/deburring the ends of wires after they have been cut. Insert the wire end into the small cup tip and rotate the handle back and forth between your fingers. You can buy wire rounders either individually or in sets with different-sized cups.

Permanent marker pens (medium and fine tips). These pens enable you to mark your tools in order to create consistent-sized loops and make custom cutters. You can also use the permanent marker to darken the silver recesses and thus avoid using chemical patinas.

CHAPTER FOUR

Basic Techniques

HOW TO WORK WITH METAL CLAY

The metal clay comes wrapped in cellophane, inside a resealable bag, so you can store it and prolong its use. As you work, make sure you wrap the excess clay with the cellophane and place it back in the bag. In order to preserve the malleability of the metal clay, it must be handled as little as possible, so it is good practice to have all the tools needed ready before opening the packet of clay.

Please note: If you work in a warm environment the clay will dry a little faster. However, the clay can be rehydrated at different stages; just follow the instructions provided later on in this chapter in order to do so.

One of the wonderful characteristics of the clay is that you can simply roll it up while it is fresh, and start again, if at first you are not happy with a shape or texture. If you change your mind once the clay has dried, but has not been fired, it is also possible to reconstitute the clay and start again!

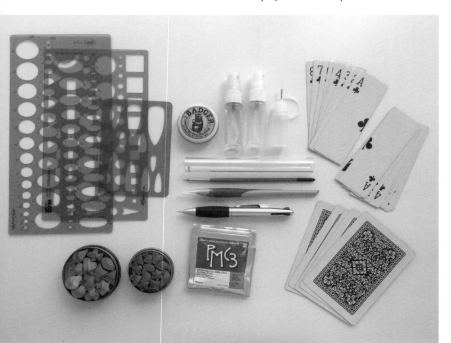

Basic Metal Clay Kit

- Olive oil or Badger Balm.
- Work mat.
- Roller.
- Depth cards/slats.
- Needle tool.
- Geometric template or cutters.
- Small tube cutter (0.75mm ferrule).

Colour-coded thickness slats.

HOW TO ROLL A PLAIN SHEET OF CLAY 0.75MM THICK

To do this you will need:

- Smooth work surface (in order to roll an even thickness).
- Work mat (a piece of Teflon, playing card, or plastic sleeve).
- Roller.
- Depth cards/thickness slats (number 3, or corresponding colour slats).
- Olive oil or Badger Balm.
- Metal clay.

1. Place the work mat on the work surface.

2. Set the number 3 depth cards on the work mat, leaving a gap between them.

3. Apply a drop of olive oil (or a tiny bit of Badger Balm) on the palm of your hands. Rub the excess on the roller and the work mat.

4. Open the packet of clay. Take a pea-sized pinch of clay and place it on the work mat, between the number 3 depth cards.

5. Place the roller over the pair of number 3 depth cards and clay. Firmly roll over the clay a couple of times to get a consistent thickness. The depth cards will stop the roller from compressing the clay too much.

CUTTING A SHAPE

Once you have a sheet of clay, you can proceed to cut a small shape.

You will need:

- Geometric template or cutter.
- Needle tool.
- Depth cards/thickness slats (number 3, or corresponding colour slats).

1. Straight after rolling out a sheet of clay 0.75mm thick, rest the geometric template over the number 3 depth cards/thickness slats. Your desired shape should be over the clay.

2. With the needle tool completely upright, trace the inside edge of the shape. Do not angle the needle tool as you trace the edge of the shape, as this will produce uneven, wedged edges.

3. Remove the template.

4. With the needle tool, make a cut from the edge of the shape all the way to the edge of the clay; this will facilitate removing the excess clay.

5. Remove excess clay, wrap and return back to the resealable bag.

MAKING AN OPENING FOR A BAIL

Following immediately from the previous steps, you can make a small opening to accommodate a bail, or another finding, using a small tube cutter (0.75 ferrule)

1. Hold the tube cutter upright, 2mm in from the edge of the metal clay shape you just made.

2. Press the tube into the clay, turn it between your fingers a couple of times, and lift. The small divot of clay should come away inside the tube. Use a pin to push the bit of excess clay out and return it to the packet. If the divot stays in place, don't worry, as you will be able to push it out easily once the clay shape has dried.

3. Do not try to clean the edges of the clay at this stage; you will be able do so after it has dried.

4. Allow the clay shape to dry (either naturally or heat assisted).

HOW TO ROLL A TEXTURED SHEET OF CLAY 0.75MM THICK

Metal clay captures textures beautifully, giving you scope for a wide variety of designs. It is important to remember that you must texture the clay first, and then cut out the shape you want, otherwise the shape will distort.

For this you will need:
- Smooth work surface (in order to roll an even thickness).
- Work mat (a piece of Teflon, playing card, or plastic sleeve).
- Roller.
- Depth cards/thickness slats (number 3 and 4, or corresponding colour slats).
- Shallow texture plate.
- Acrylic block.
- Toothbrush.
- Olive oil or Badger Balm.
- Metal clay.

1. Place the work mat on the work surface.

2. Set the number 4 depth cards on the work mat, leaving a gap between them.

3. Apply a drop of olive oil (or a tiny bit of Badger Balm) on the palm of your hands and rub the excess on the roller and the work mat.

4. Open the packet of clay. Take a pea-sized pinch of clay and place it on the work mat, between the number 4 depth cards.

5. Place the roller over the pair of number 4 depth cards and clay. Firmly roll over the clay a couple of times to get a consistent thickness. The depth cards will stop the roller from compressing the clay too much.

6. Remove the number 4 depth cards.

7. Place the number 3 depth cards at either side of the clay.

8. Lubricate the texture plate by applying a drop of olive oil onto a toothbrush and rubbing it over the texture plate.

9. Place the texture plate over the clay, making sure the plate rests on the number 3 depth cards.

10. Use the acrylic block to firmly press the texture plate down until it rests on the depth cards.

11. Remove the block and texture plate to reveal the impression in the clay. Sometimes the clay attaches itself to the plate. If this happens, gently peel it off and put it back on the work mat.

12. Now you can proceed to cut out a shape and make an opening for the bail or finding.

Please note that shallow textures only require one depth card difference, for instance from 4 down to 3. Deeper textures need to be thicker to start with in order to take a deeper impression, so you should start with 5 card depth and go down to 3. Some textures might need 6 cards, but always go down to 3.

FIRING CLAY

Once the clay has dried, it is ready to be fired. In order to check that all the water has evaporated, place the refined clay piece on a mirror for a few seconds. Then remove the piece. If there is no 'vapour ghost' where the piece was, the clay is dry.

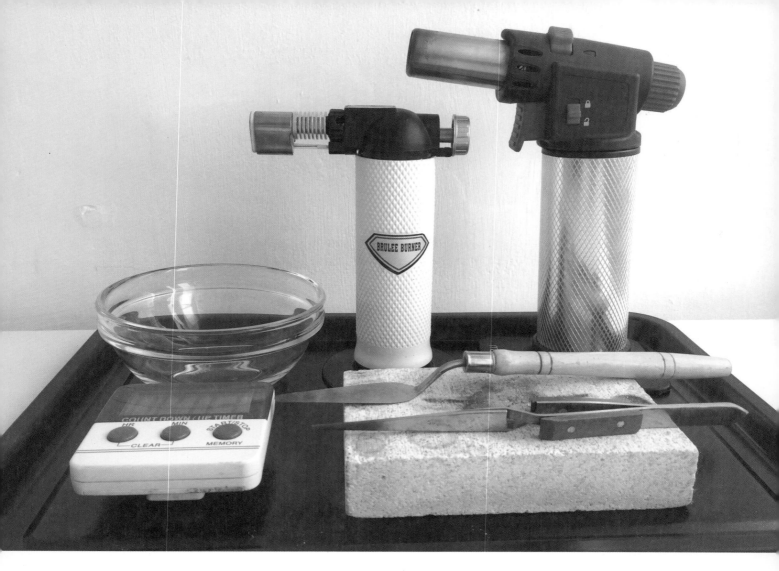

To fire the clay you will need:

Basic firing kit
- Baking tray.
- Firebrick.
- Timer.
- Blowtorch.
- Insulated reverse action tweezers.
- Small metal spatula.
- Small glass dish with water.

Safety first: goggles, apron, hair tied back, no loose clothing and a fire extinguisher.

It is important that you work in a well-ventilated area, and in a slightly darkened room, away from bright windows, so you can properly observe the colour variations during the firing process.

1. Place the refined piece of clay onto the firebrick.

2. Ignite the blowtorch and with a circular motion let the flame go over the piece. DO NOT place the blowtorch directly above the piece as this will create a feedback loop. Instead, hold the blowtorch to the side and at a slight angle. Make sure you are in a comfortable position; two minutes is a long time when you are 'drawing' small circles with a blowtorch in your hand.

3. A little smoke and a flame will appear as the binder burns off.

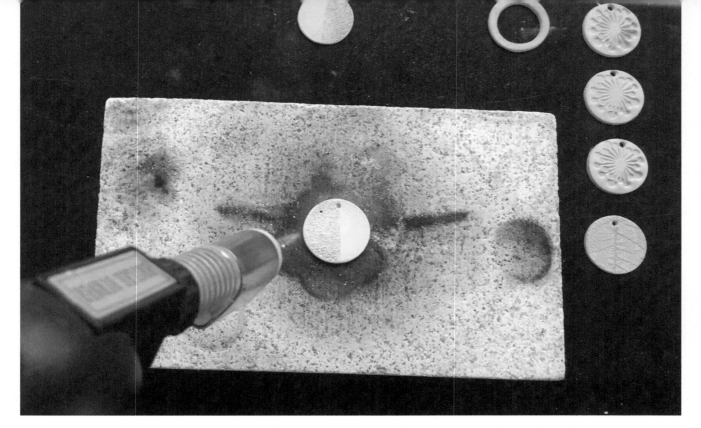

4. You will see an orange glow appear where the flame meets the clay. Then the piece will start to turn a 'pale salmon' colour.

Please note that the piece might buckle up a little, but it should go down again on its own once the firing is finished.

5. Start the timer as the piece reaches the 'pale salmon' colour. In order to ensure proper sintering, try to hold the clay's temperature to a constant 'pale salmon' for two minutes.

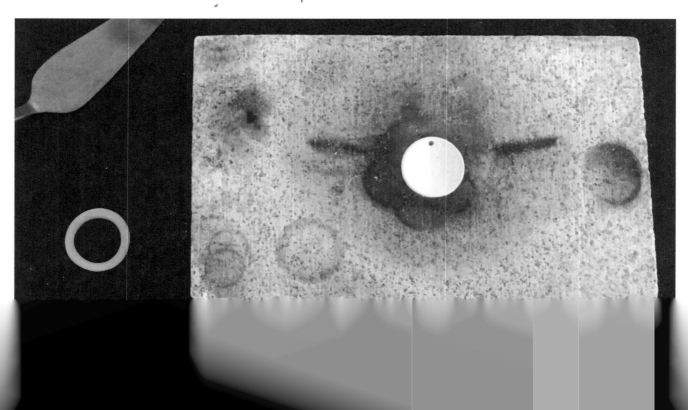

If the piece starts to look bright red or silvery, pull back the torch a little, since this indicates the piece is beginning to melt.

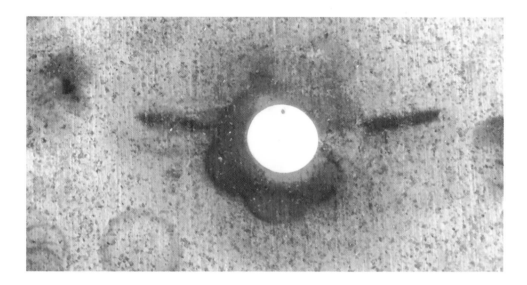

However, if the piece is looking dull grey it is not hot enough, so bring the blowtorch a little closer.

6. Once the two minutes are up, turn the blowtorch off and place it in front of you, as far away as possible.

7. Slide the spatula under the piece (away from you), resting the tweezers on top of the piece to prevent it from sliding off. DO NOT TRY TO PICK THE PIECE UP WITH THE TWEEZERS as this can make it flip, USE THE SPATULA instead.

Cool the piece down by carefully placing it in the cold water dish (this is known as quenching). The piece cools instantly, but always check the temperature of the water first. If the water is cold, the piece will be cold; if the water feels hot, do not touch the metal piece.

If for whatever reason the firing process is interrupted, do not worry. All you need to do is heat the piece up to the 'pale salmon' colour again and start the two minutes count afresh.

What to do when things go wrong:
The most common mistake happens when the clay is overheated and it begins to melt. The surface starts to look shiny and rough (this is called reticulation). Depending on the degree of reticulation, you can either embrace it (reticulated silver can be attractive), or you can apply a hammered finish to the piece, thus flattening the surface.

REHYDRATING CLAY

Silver metal clay is made up of fine silver particles, organic binder and water. As you work with metal clay, the water contained in the binder slowly evaporates (in a warm environment this happens faster). You will notice this around the edges, as the clay appears 'cracked'. When this happens, simply follow these steps:

1. Place the clay between a piece of folded cellophane wrapper.

2. Roll the clay out as thinly as possible.

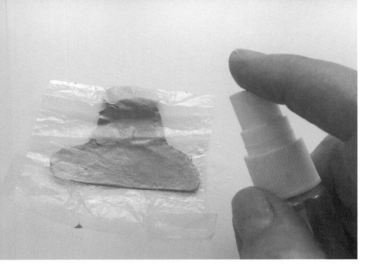 

3. Peel open one half of the cellophane.

4. Spray once or spread a drop of clean water over the surface of the clay.

5. Fold the clay in half, using the cellophane, and then peel off one side of the cellophane..

6. Spread another drop of clean water over the surface of the clay.

7. Fold the clay in half using the cellophane and peel the cellophane back, and then repeat this. With your fingers, squeeze the clay gently over the cellophane to work the water in.

8. Allow the clay to rest for a few minutes before working with it.

RECONSTITUTING CLAY

There are times when the clay dries out completely and becomes a solid mass, or we change our mind about a piece of dry unfired clay. When this happens, the clay can be brought back to life with the process below.

You will need:
Safety first: goggles and face mask

- Electric coffee/herb grinder, or small smooth pestle and mortar (both designated for metal clay use only!).
- Stainless steel replacement mesh filter for coffee, or ultra-fine mesh sieve (like an oil/soup skimmer spoon).
- Sheet of A4 paper.
- CMC powder (used for cake decorations).
- Small spray bottle with water.
- Small clean container.
- Small spatula.

1. Place the hardened clay in the grinder (or pestle and mortar). and pulverise

2. Working over the sheet of paper, pour the clay powder onto the mesh/sieve to separate out the bigger particles (use the spatula to help). Set the big particles apart.

3. Transfer the fine clay powder to the container.

4. Add a tiny pinch of CMC to the clay powder and mix well.

5. To the mix of clay and CMC add one spray of water.

6. Mix well with the spatula. The clay will look crumbly.

7. Add a second spray of water and mix well. The clay should start coming together, forming a lump as you stir.

8. If needed, add a third spray of water, but be careful, as it is easy to overwater the clay and turn it into a paste!

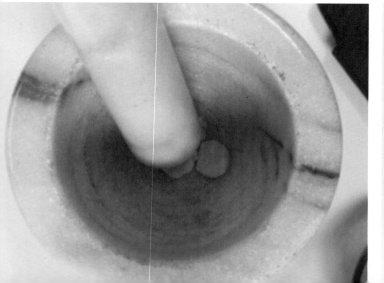

9. Wrap the lump of clay in a piece of cellophane and store in the original resealable bag.

10. Let it sit for an hour, then it will be ready to use.

SILVERSMITHING BASIC TECHNIQUES

Making jump rings

You will need:
- Sterling wire 1mm x 200mm.
- Flush cutters.
- Three-stepped forming pliers (various sizes available), or a firm tube or straw to form the jump rings on.
- Alternatively, round concave pliers (to make different size jump ring).

1. Using three-stepped forming pliers. The nose of these pliers has two different sides. One side of the nose is long, uniform and covered in plastic tubing to prevent marring the metal. The other side of the nose is a mandrel with three different diameters. Select the desired size mandrel. Wrap the wire over the barrel tightly to form a spring. Feed the wire as you turn the pliers. Every coil in the spring will make a jump ring.

2. Remove spring from the pliers.

3. Using the flush cutters, separate the rings by cutting across the spring one section at a time, on the same spot and in a straight line. The inner diameter (ID) of the jump rings will correspond to the size of the mandrel you use to make them.

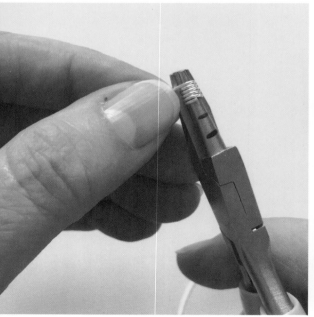
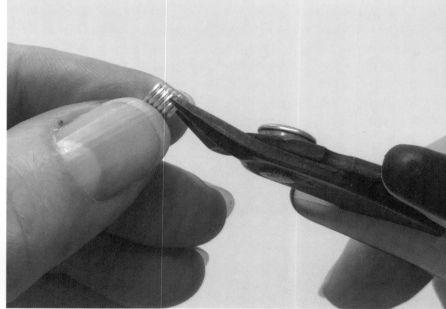

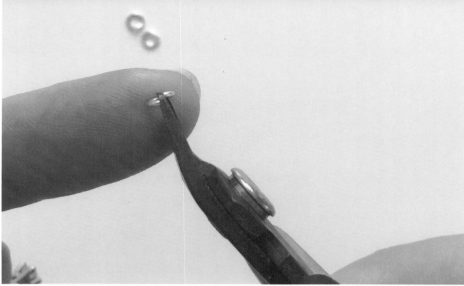

4. Your jump rings should have one end of the wire completely flat, and the other with a small apex. You can snip the apex with the cutters, but be careful to only cut off the apex (a tiny amount of silver).

Please note: do not throw away the silver clippings, save any bits in a container. They soon add up, and you can sell them for scrap, or ball them up and use as decorative elements.

Opening and closing a jump ring

You will need:
- Chain-nose pliers.
- Bent-nose pliers.

1. Hold the jump ring with the bent-nose pliers in your non-dominant hand. You should be able to see the opening of the ring.

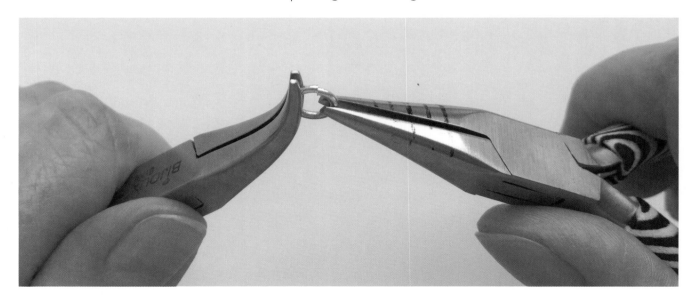

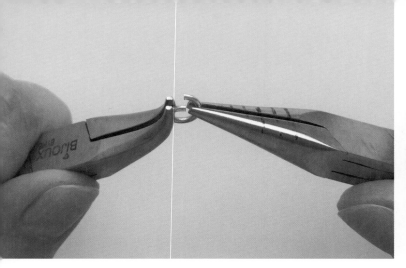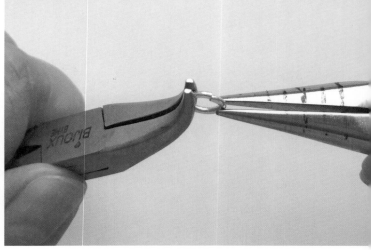

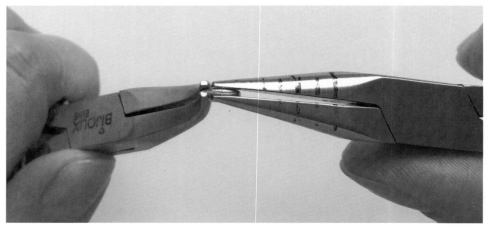

54. Grasp the other side of the ring with the chain-nose pliers and gently push away from you, in a north–south direction, to open the ring. Never pull apart the ring apart so the circle gets larger!

55. To close, reverse the action, pushing the far side towards you.

56. Adjust if necessary, by gently pressing the ring together with the chain-nose pliers.

Balling wire

Safety first: Protect your eyes, tie your hair back (if applicable) and avoid loose clothing.

You will need: basic firing kit

1. Stand the blowtorch on the baking tray and place the glass dish with water directly below the tip of the blowtorch's nozzle.

2. Hold the wire with the reverse action tweezers, and at a 90-degree angle to the tweezers.

3. Ignite the torch and lower the bottom end of the wire into the flame, just in front of the pale blue cone of the flame (which is the hottest part of the flame).

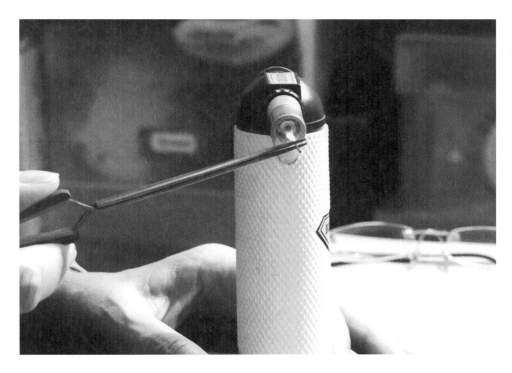

4. The tip of the wire will start to melt and draw up into a ball. The longer the wire is exposed to the flame, the larger the ball will be. However, if allowed to get too big, the ball will drop off into the water dish.

5. Once you have a pleasing ball end, quench the wire in the water dish.

WORK-HARDENING METAL

Safety first: Protect your eyes with goggles

You will need:
- Steel block.
- Nylon hammer.
- Cork mat.

When metal is heated it becomes softer. In order to restore the metal's rigidity, it is necessary to work-harden it. Simply place the piece of metal or wire on the steel block and gently tap it with the nylon hammer (sometimes it is necessary to use a chasing hammer instead). The nylon hammer will not deform the metal. Test rigidity of the metal after every other hammer tap.

CHAPTER FIVE

Aspects of Design

DESIGNING AND SELLING JEWELLERY

Jewellery design is an extensive field, but we can condense down some important aspects into manageable and useful points.

The projects in this book will guide you through different techniques, illustrate design possibilities to ignite your creativity, and enable you to combine the finished pieces into more complex designs.

When you design and make a jewellery piece for sale, bear in mind the following:

Who is your audience? Think about the style, lifestyle, gender, age, location, education, profession, household income, spending habits, marital/family situation, or religion of your target customer. All of these will help you to work out what types of piece you should make, who will buy them, and how much they will be willing to pay for them.

What is the concept behind the design? What inspired you? Are you telling a story? How will the piece express this? Are you using a single element (for example a butterfly) or a combination (a butterfly and a flower)? How would you describe your inspiration (nature, sea, etc.)?

Include elements to tie the design by the use of consistent materials and finishes, for instance a mirror finish and oxidised textures. Adhere to a particular colour palette; use patinas to create an antique look, a rainbow finish, or a dramatic matt black and shiny silver contrast. Repeat shapes and forms, for example decreasing size elements, or use multiple pieces of the same size (remember, odd numbers of pieces are more visually appealing).

Develop defining techniques and designs to stand out from the crowd: be original! Focus on and carry detail: make sure that every

mark on your pieces is intentional and not accidental. Finish all your pieces to the highest standard: people will remember you and your work if you do, and they will be happy to recommend you to others. That's how you build a brand.

RECORDING YOUR IDEAS AND DESIGNS: SKETCHBOOKS AND JOURNALS

A visual journal allows you to explore ideas in depth as you record and collate information and images, enabling you to develop a personal design language.

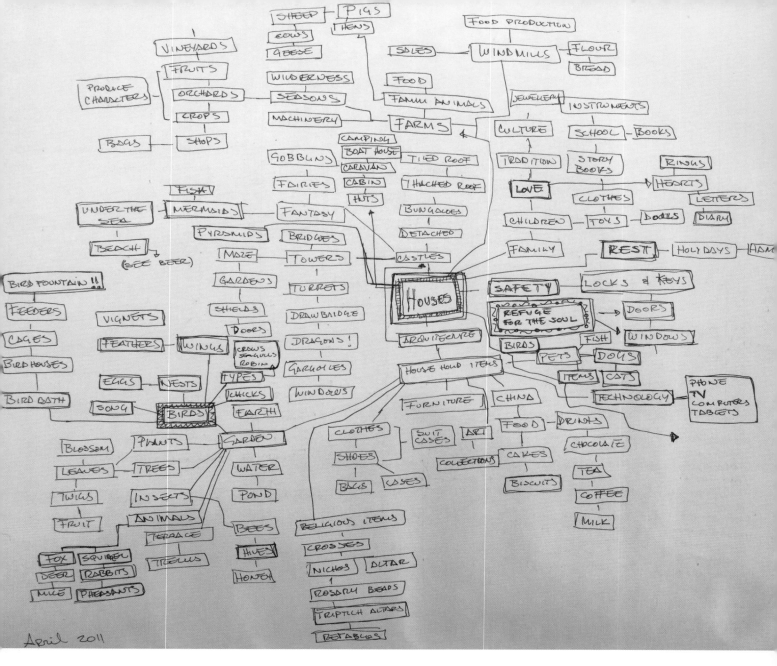

Spidergram for 'Houses'.

A good way to explore an idea is by creating a spidergram (a word association exercise). Simply write down a key word, for instance 'flower', in the centre of a page, then list out everything you associate with that word: think both literally and laterally. Themes will develop, for example: flower – leaf; insect – butterfly – ladybird, and so on. Collect assorted images related to your chosen subject (Pinterest is great for this!).

Make notes of what you like and do not like, and develop your own design (DO NOT COPY THE WORK OF OTHERS). Explore your ideas and think how you could turn them into earrings, pendants, necklaces, and bracelets (please note: rings are not covered in this book). All these pieces will be tied in by a theme and will therefore become a cohesive collection.

A sketchbook enables you to explore and record ideas and observations. A quick drawing (or a note) is as important as a detailed rendering of a piece. Inspiration and ideas are ephemeral, so always have paper and pen/pencil with you to capture them. Do

'Birdsong'. From simple sketches to finished necklace.

not feel that you have to be good at drawing. The important thing is that the sketch or note makes sense to you, and that you are able to develop the idea into a piece of jewellery.

Technical journals chronicle the development and elaboration process, areas that require particular attention, materials, suppliers and outcomes (both good and bad), as well as health and safety information.

Technical journals are invaluable for jewellery makers in general, and metal clay artists in particular, since we need to record so much more additional information, from breaking down the construction stages, to identifying the necessary elements to elaborate a design.

ASPECTS OF DESIGN

When we design a piece of jewellery, we hope to create something memorable. In order to do so, we must pay particular attention to the following aspects of design:

Lines

Lines are part of the visual language of a piece, and it is therefore helpful to understand the messages lines typically convey and how they are perceived.

Line weight: The weight of a line, how wide or narrow it is, plays a part in design. It can be used for emphasis (thick), as an accent (thin), or for direction (dark to light), guiding the focus from one area to another.

Line quality: The quality of the lines in a design define the visual language of a piece. Sketchy, lightly etched lines suggest softness. Deep lines, by contrast, are dominant and commanding. Uniform lines convey purpose, energy and rhythm.

Line as texture: Patterns emerge as lines of different shape, size, weight and quality combine or outline geometric shapes. Lines that cross draw attention and become focal points. Random lines convey spontaneity. Uniform lines give an impression of order and rhythm. Small linear patterns can easily blend into the background, whilst patterns with deep, wide lines stand out.

Orientation of a design

Orientation is an important part of the visual language of a design, and contributes to the message we wish to convey. The three main orientations (or axes) of form in design are linear (either horizontal or vertical), curved, or angled. All other axis arrangements are variations of these.

Horizontal designs have a calming and stable quality. They help

Jurassic collection inspired by Beer village and the Jurassic Coast.

to direct the eye from left to right and act as an anchor for other elements.

Vertical designs provide strength and stability to the visual language of a piece. Vertical designs feel more natural and tend to be more flattering because they draw attention from top to bottom.

Curved, circular and spiral designs have an active, organic and feminine quality. Shallow curves suggest warmth, softness, and a relaxing motion, whilst tight and steep curves convey energy, speed and vibrancy. The inclusion of curves in a piece imbues movement to the design.

Angular lines denote movement, are dynamic and are more masculine. By varying the sharpness and intervals of the angles they can convey energy, anger, excitement or dynamism.

Diagonal designs suggest action, movement and direction, depending on the sharpness and distance between the angles. Multiple diagonal lines give an illusion of perspective, or depth, when they share the same meeting point (as in one-point perspective), suggesting a foreground and a background.

Movement

Movement presents an opportunity to create rhythm, flow or drama in a piece. Movement in design can be achieved in two ways:

visual and physical (kinetic). Kinetic elements are moving parts in a jewellery piece, and they can be simple or complex.

Simple kinetic elements are set in motion by natural body movement, or an external force like the wind, for example dangling earrings, or spinning elements.

Complex kinetic elements incorporate wind-up mechanisms, spring-action movements, magnets, batteries or cranks to set the piece or decorative elements in motion.

Visual movement uses design elements to create a path that guides the eye through a piece of jewellery. This visual path can be uniform, fluid, gradual, dynamic or ordinary.

Uniform: contains predictable design elements, placed at regular intervals, allowing the viewer to anticipate repetition. For example, alternate light and dark areas, repetitive patterns, graded size-shape-texture-volume, or geometric combinations.

Fluid: slowly guides the eye through the design by the use of soft curves and edges, organic lines and round elements. Textured transitions are subtle, graded, and the overall design is harmonious.

Gradual: guides the eye to a focal point, building interest as it progresses. The design develops gradually in steps or stages, and has continuity. For example, size transitions from small to large, texture progression from mirror finish to rough area, all of which converge on the focal point.

Dynamic: involves a sudden change in the design elements, creating contrast. Sharp lines and edges are present. Bright colours are involved, either in contrasting or complementary hues. Size difference is emphasised and bold patterns are included to create a greater visual impact.
Note that over-use of any of the above elements could give the impression of chaos, so be careful.

Ordinary: is uncomplicated, understated and predictable. The intervals between elements are small, textures are subtle, lines are horizontal, curves are soft. A single focal point might be included in the piece, or none at all.

Minimalism
Minimalist design is uncomplicated and elegant. It may incorporate

bold elements, and purposeful details, but these are simplified or stylised. The well-defined lines, shapes and forms demand perfection in craftsmanship (there is nowhere to hide!). Patterns are sleek, clean and organised, often geometric or futuristic, which is part of its sophisticated appeal.

There is a fine line between minimalist design, and uniform and boring jewellery. This is evident when the energy of a piece is so low that it creates no excitement at all. It happens when lines are too simplistic, with little or no visual interest. The relationship between elements is lacking, and the design has too much 'dead space'. The directional lines guide you away from the composition, the patterns are too predictable, there are no areas of excitement, contrast or energy, and the piece's focal point fails to hold interest, or is devoid of meaning. A piece with these characteristics denotes both poor design and craftsmanship.

Form, size and scale, and balance

Form, as a design element, refers to the arrangement of parts and shapes, and the use of space. Two-dimensional pieces have height and width, whilst three-dimensional forms have height, width, depth and volume. Form can be organic (with random, naturally flowing, ruffled lines and edges), linear (sharp, hard edges and flat surfaces), geometric (regular shapes creating repetitive patterns, like honeycombs), and structured (planned, symmetrical and well organised).

The harmony, unity and cohesiveness of design elements depend on how light plays on the surface, how size and scale relate to each other and the wearer, how space and volume are perceived, and whether the orientation of the elements is balanced and pleasing.

Light interacts with the edges, contours, surfaces and details of a piece, and can add a sense of volume. A shiny mirror finish reflects the light, but textured surfaces diffuse it, particularly when patinas are used to create contrast or a 'chiaroscuro' effect. Rounded forms or smooth contours produce a gradual light transition, whilst sharp angles and hard edges create a strong, sudden light change. Concave shapes and negative spaces (pierced, cut or open areas between objects or elements) cast shadows and add interest. Large, solid convex shapes and surfaces tend to reflect more light.

Size and scale influence the perception of a piece. For instance, large elements draw attention, whilst small elements recede and are less noticeable. The close proximity of two very different-sized elements will emphasise their dimensions, adding dramatic flair, although careful planning is required since it does not take much to throw a piece off balance. A sense of volume can be achieved by the use of large forms or large areas of negative space (gaps).

Jewellery design must be functional as well as aesthetically pleasing. The focal point (the highlight of the piece, usually larger and attention grabbing), needs to be balanced in order to prevent the piece from leaning to one side or tipping forward, and the piece should also be comfortable to wear. The focal point does not necessarily have to be in the centre of the design, but should be a well-defined area of the piece.

Supportive elements never compete with the focal point; instead they should add excitement and contrast, and must be organised to achieve balance and harmony.

Balance and focus. Balance is the distribution of visual weight between the elements of a piece. The distribution of elements can be: symmetrical (same number of elements are arranged equally on both sides of the focal point), or asymmetrical (elements differ in shape, size, or arrangement on each side).

SELLING YOUR JEWELLERY

Are you intending to sell your jewellery? If so, please note that some countries require you to register with the Assay Office (or equivalent) when selling precious metals, as is the case in the UK.

It is good practice to diversify price points by creating pieces that carry the same elements of design, flowers, hearts, stars, etc., in different sizes. Scale up too! Make a few larger statement pieces, which will be more pricey (display them prominently). You might sell fewer of them, but they are your desirable pieces and they will spark interest.

Highest perceived value possible: sign your pieces, include a small distinctive embellishment unique to you. Hidden words and messages only visible to the wearer are very appealing, as are collections tied to a good cause (generate good karma!). Use packaging that tells a story.

Allow 'breathing' space when you display your jewellery. A common mistake is to 'overload' a table or cabinet with random jewellery pieces thrown together. This gives the impression of mass-produced, inexpensive jewellery. Instead, cultivate an image that celebrates craftsmanship, and carefully curates one-of-a-kind pieces (think art gallery rather than jumble sale).

Encourage collectability and develop desirability: create stacking elements, layered looks (combination sets of two or more elements), mix and match elements with other pieces. Create one-of-a-kind collection pieces.

If you are selling, display pieces as sets: earrings, necklaces and bracelets with the same theme or design in the same section (bundle up!). This way, potential customers will be inspired to 'collect' your jewellery to complete the set.

Identify the features of your jewellery: it is lightweight, made of fine silver which does not tarnish, etc. Also identify the benefits: comfortable to wear, easy to maintain, etc.

Ask for the sale!

Buying jewellery is an emotional decision. Create a positive environment and pleasant experience to facilitate it! Engage in a little conversation, but do not overwhelm your customers!

Don't hesitate to say **'shall I wrap this for you?'** or something similar. A little polite help can make the difference.

Offer to personalise items for a fee. Fingerprint jewellery is particularly suitable for this. Also, pieces that incorporate a favourite or empowering word can be personalised.

Remember, commissions carry a premium price, since they might be difficult to sell to someone else, and it is also advisable to ask for a 50 per cent deposit.

HOW TO PRICE YOUR JEWELLERY

Record in your technical journal how pieces are made: type of clay, techniques/instructions, templates and textures, size before and after firing, thickness, refining process (before and after firing), firing schedule, shrinkage, finishes, problems, elaboration time, designated SKU (stock keeping unit – the alphanumeric code you create for inventory and ordering purposes), etc. This information will enable you to recreate a piece, to work out costs and to set a price. Remember to include hallmarking fees, postage and packaging, and that your time should also be included (decide how much you would like to get per hour or day – but be realistic).

The most basic pricing formula to use:

Materials + overheads + time = COST
Cost x 2 = WHOLESALE
Wholesale x 2 = RETAIL MAP (Minimum Advertised Price)

However, particularly with the Internet, things are now more complicated. In determining a price you will need to take account of the design and its uniqueness; the target customer; the competition; and also what the market will bear. Where you are selling the items will also have an impact.

YOUR STORY

Identify what inspires you, and what techniques you use and like to use when you create a piece. What is your subject matter or theme? Nature, houses, fairy tales, etc. Is there an underlying message to your collection? Like conservation or friendship. How does your background or personal story relate? Do you live in the countryside or near the sea?

How to use your story:
Your story will be a source of conversation with customers, a source for interviews, press releases, website, blog posts, social media, emails, brochure, packaging, booth and table signage.

CHAPTER SIX

Minimalist Earrings

LEARNING HOW TO make a simple hammered disc will enable you to create many different pieces in a variety of styles. It will also provide the skills needed to fix a piece if (and when) things go wrong, which happens to all of us at some point.

The project's steps will guide you through the entire making process, and the design options section will provide you with

suggestions for multiple pieces. Although for this first project I used a disc, you can, in fact, use any geometric shape.

Have fun and don't forget to breathe!

Materials:
- PMC3 5g
- Basic metal clay kit (see basic techniques section).
- Small tube cutters (ferrules) or a thin straw.
- 15mm circle cutter or geometric template and needle tool.
- Basic firing kit (see basic techniques section).
- Fish hook earrings.

Forming:
1. Roll out the clay to 2 cards thick (0.50mm).

2. Cut the clay with the 15mm circle cutter, or by using the 15mm circle opening on the geometric template and the fine needle tool (ensure the tool is perfectly upright as you cut). The edges might look a little rough at this stage, but do not try to fix them now; wait until the piece has dried before doing so.

3. Cut a second disc as above.

4. Store excess clay back in the packet.

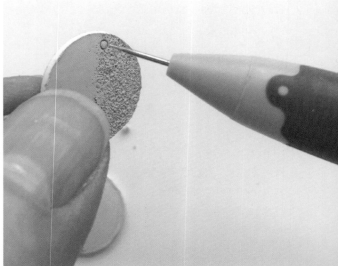

5. Use the 1mm tube cutter to create an opening on each disc for the earring hooks. Just hold the tube upright by the coloured end and push the metal bit into the clay, approximately 2mm from the edge. Wiggle/twist the tube a little to release. The small clay divot should come away inside the tube; take it out with a pin or wire, and return it to the lump of clay. Occasionally the divot does not come out, in which case leave it in place until the piece is dry, and then gently push it out with a pin (store the divots).

6. Allow the pieces to dry.

Refining and Firing:

1. Check the pieces have dried completely, by placing them over a mirror. If the pieces are dry, there will be no vapour left on the

mirror. If there is 'ghosting', allow them to dry a little longer.

2. Once the pieces have dried, run your finger over the edges to dislodge any flakes, and then gently run the nail file (use the least coarse side) in one direction along the edges. Note that if you try to 'sand away' a blemish with the nail file, you could distort the shape. It is much easier to refine a piece in its clay form; it takes little effort and the shavings can be reconstituted into clay (see Basic Techniques chapter). Another way to refine the edge is with a damp makeup wedge or a wet wipe. If using either the wedge or wipe, work fast and make sure to only touch the area in need of fixing, as prolonged contact with a damp surface can distort the piece.

3. Use a round mini-file or a toothpick to tidy up the inside of the holes.

Firing

1. Fire each disc for two minutes. In order to ensure proper sintering, try to hold the clay's temperature to a constant 'pale salmon' (if the piece starts to look bright red or silvery, pull back the torch a little, since this indicates the piece is beginning to melt).

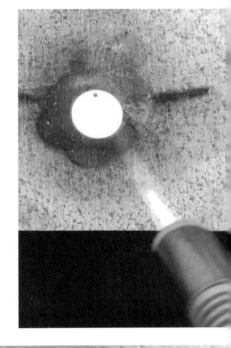

2. Once a disc has been fired, slide a spatula under it (away from you) and, if necessary, rest the tweezers on top of the piece to prevent it from sliding off. Cool the pieces down by carefully placing them in a dish of cold water (this is known as quenching). Do not try to pick them up with the tweezers as this can make them flip; use the spatula instead. The pieces cool instantly, but always check the temperature of the water first. If the water is cold, the pieces will be cold, but if the water feels hot, do not touch the metal pieces.

Hammered finish:

1. Place the rubber/nylon block on a paper towel. Take the discs out of the water and place them on the block. The metal discs will look a little frosted: this is the natural look of silver. To bring out the sheen of the metal, use a damp wire brush and firmly brush each disc in one direction. Repeat on the other side and on the edges. The silver will now have a satin finish. If any of the frosting still shows, use the damp brush again.

2. Select the side that is going to be hammered. Place a disc on the steel block and, using the ball end of the

hammer, gently tap the surface of the disc. Indentations will begin to cover the surface. Make sure the markings are evenly distributed by rotating the disc periodically.

3. Repeat with the second disc.

Note that the hammered finish is easy to achieve, looks great, and can rescue a piece that has gone wrong, for instance if the disc begins to melt, the surface has a blemish (like a blister), or if we change our minds about a texture.

It is important to remember that hammering will harden the metal, but also make it brittle, so it might be necessary to reheat it to a pale salmon colour, quench, and then continue hammering in order to prevent breaking the piece (this applies to pieces that have been textured previously, have been polished, or have been worn).

Polish and Finishing:

1. You can bring the disc to a mirror finish with an agate burnisher. The smooth agate surface glides over the silver, compressing it, and bringing the metal to a lovely high sheen without leaving tool marks (avoid using the tip of the tool or you will create grooves!). Note that burnishing and hammering cause the metal to displace a little, creating sharp edges which can cause discomfort. To fix this, gently run an emery board at a 30-degree angle along the top and bottom edges.

2. If desired, a Liver of Sulphur patina can be applied to enhance the dents (see *A Touch of Colour* chapter).

3. Use a soft polishing cloth to bring the piece to a mirror finish.

4. Push open the bail's ring, or jump ring, with the pliers (hold the ring with bent-nose pliers and push open with chain-nose pliers).

5. Insert disc on the ring and push closed carefully so no tool marks are left on the piece. Ensure the opening on the bail is on the reverse of the silver piece.

Design Options

Earrings:

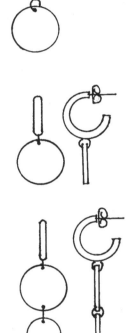

Pendants:

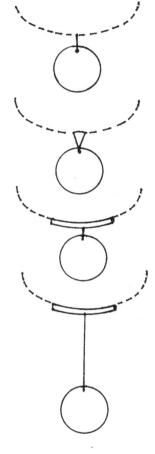

Necklaces:

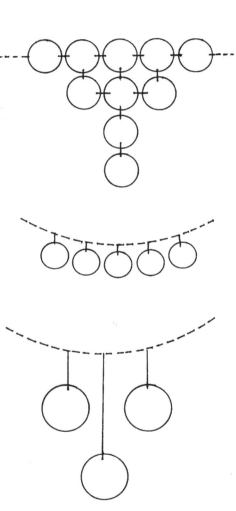

Bracelets:

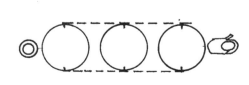

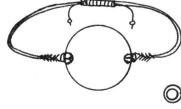

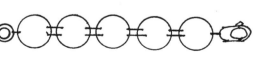

CHAPTER SEVEN

Lacuna Pendant

LACUNA IS DEFINED as a blank space, a small cavity, a pit, a missing part or a discontinuity in an anatomical structure. Beautiful pieces with either an architectural structure or an organic feel can be made by removing material, creating spaces (both regular and irregular),

pits and dimples. The gaps can vary in size, shape and form, from decreasing circles, to uniform hexagons skilfully positioned to evoke a beehive, or a stained glass rosette. This style of jewellery is light and very attractive.

In this project we will explore different ways to create decorative gaps, cavities and dimples with an embossing pen and custom-made mini cutters. We will also look at important design considerations specific to a lacuna piece.

Let's get started! First of all, let's look at how to make your own mini cutters

You will need:
- Assorted electrical terminal wire connectors (ferrules).
- Round-nose pliers.
- Chain-nose pliers.
- A fine Sharpie.
- A little patience!

Wire connectors are your friends! They are really useful as they are perfect coloured-coded mini tube cutters in assorted sizes. And the soft metal the connectors are made from enables us to modify them with pliers and a little patience.

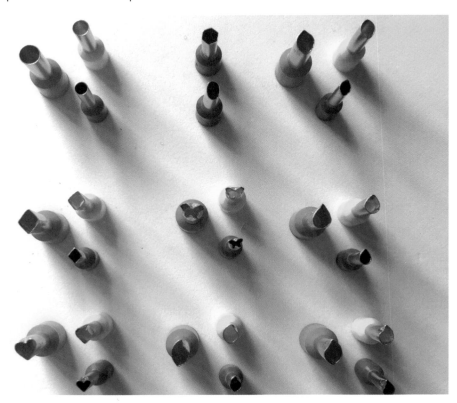

1. The first thing to do is to mark one side of the nose of both the chain-nose pliers and the round-nose pliers. This simple tip will help you not only with this project, but with jewellery-making in general. Simply find the middle of the nose (you don't have to measure, just eyeball it) and draw a horizontal line across both sides of the pliers' nose.

2. Now divide each section in half again (you will then have three horizontal lines).

3. Repeat twice more in each section (you will have eight marks). These markings will enable you to have consistent sizing.

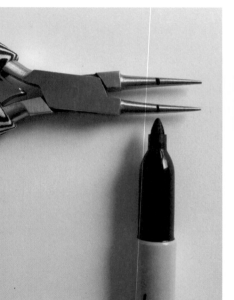 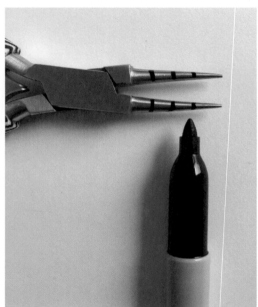 

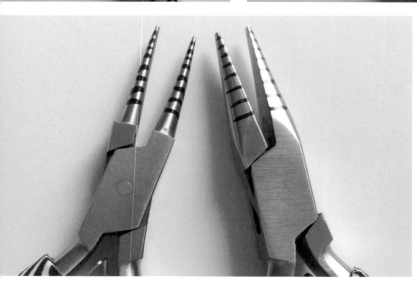

If your markings are askew, you can erase them with nail polish remover, and then start again. Please note: as you work with your pliers, the markings will partially fade away or disappear completely, so touch them up as necessary.

Start with the largest wire connector and, as you become more familiar with the process, you can then work with the smaller ones.

To make an oval with curved sides: Close the nose of the round-nose pliers and insert into the tube up to the third mark, then gently prise apart the handles of the pliers but without forcing them. The tube will elongate, creating a perfect oval. To create smaller ovals, insert the round-nose pliers into the next size down tube, line up to the second mark and gently prise apart the handles as before. Repeat the process with a smaller tube, and line up with the first mark.

The instructions below relate to the largest wire connector.
To make an oval with flat sides: Place the tube inside the nose of the chain-nose pliers and gently squeeze a little to slightly flatten the sides. Release the tube, turn it around and gently squeeze again to even out the shape. If you need to round the curves, close the nose of the round-nose pliers and insert into the tube, move the tube up the round nose as far as it will go without forcing it. This will also even out the curves on both sides.

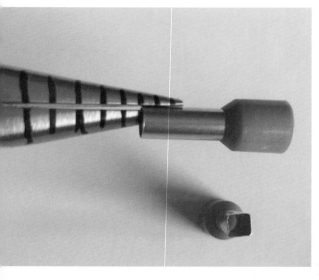

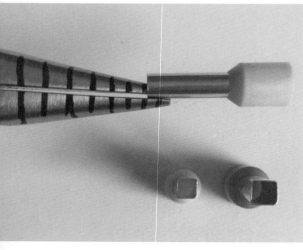

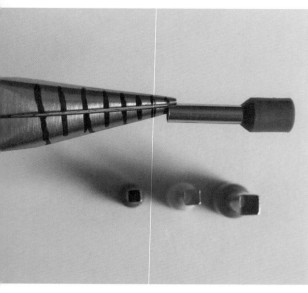

To make a square cutter: Insert one side of the chain-nose pliers into the tube, line the tube up to the third mark from the tip, and gently squeeze. This will flatten that part of the metal tube. This is the first side of your square. Now position the pliers on the round section next to the flat part and gently squeeze to create the next side of the square. Work your way around the rest of the tube and adjust the sides if necessary.

To make the medium-sized cutter: line up the tube with the second mark from the tip of your pliers, and with the first mark to make the smallest size. If at any point things go wrong, don't worry. Simply insert one side of the round-nose pliers into the misshapen tube as far as it will go, and gently turn in one direction. The tube will recover its original shape.

To make a pentagon cutter: Insert one side of the chain-nose pliers into the tube, line the tube up to the second mark from the tip, and gently squeeze. This will flatten that part of the metal tube. This is the first side of your pentagon. Now position the pliers on the round section next to the flat part and gently squeeze to create the next side of the pentagon. Work your way round the rest of the tube and adjust the sides if necessary.

To make the medium-sized cutter: line up the tube with the first mark from the tip of your pliers, and with the very tip to make the smallest size.

To make a hexagon: Hexagons are a little more tricky, but well worth the effort!

As before, insert one side of the chain-nose pliers into the tube, line the tube almost up to the second mark from the tip, and gently squeeze. This will flatten that part of the metal tube. This is the first side of your hexagon. Now position the pliers on the round section opposite to the flat part and gently squeeze to create the next side of the hexagon. You will now have two flat parallel sections and two curves. Place the pliers halfway in to the curved section and next to one of the flat areas and gently squeeze, this will be the third side of the hexagon. Squeeze the other half of the curve

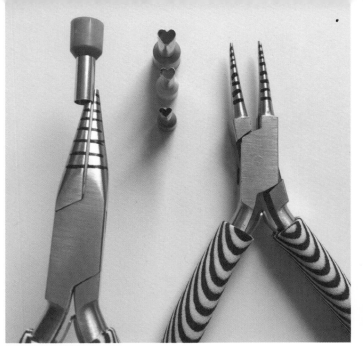
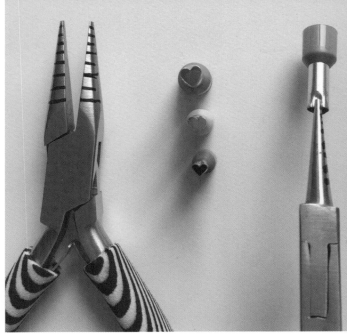
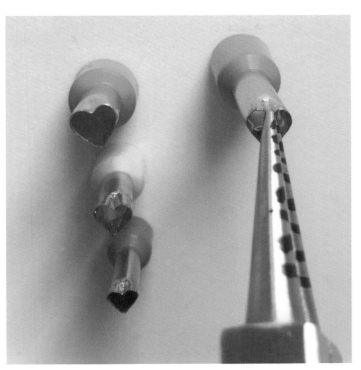
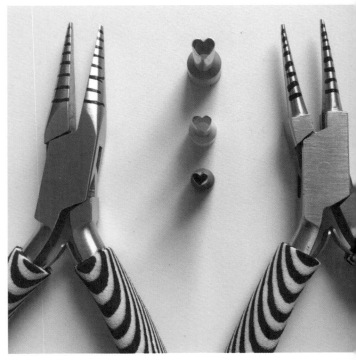

you just worked on to complete that side. Work your way round the rest of the tube and adjust the sides if necessary.

To make the medium-sized cutter: line up the tube almost to the first mark from the tip of your pliers, and with the very tip of the pliers to make the smallest size.

To make a heart: Insert the round-nose pliers into the tube, up to the second nose marking and pull towards the centre of the tube. This will create a small 'v' shape indentation. Now change to the chain-nose pliers. Directly opposite the indentation create a 'v' shape with the chain-nose pliers, by lining up to the second mark and gently squeezing one side of the 'v' and then the other. If needed, round the curved parts with the round-nose pliers. As with previous wire connectors (ferrules), move closer to the tip to make the smaller shapes.

Experiment and see how many more shapes you can create!

USING YOUR CUTTERS

When removing material from a sheet of clay, we must take into account the structural integrity of the piece. In order to compensate for the spaces created, the sheet of clay must be at least 4 depth cards thick (1mm).

Plan your design so that the openings are inside a continuous perimeter. For example, start with an oval-shaped piece of clay and then proceed to use your mini cutters to create random gaps. Or start with a geometric shape and use the round cutters in an ascending or descending size scale to add interest. A circle with a triangular or irregular opening at the base looks very attractive.

The ball ends of an embossing pen can also create interesting lacuna patterns. You can vary the depth and size of the dimples and even use them to perforate the wet clay!

If your design includes gaps that breach the perimeter, then make sure there are no sharp edges and points that can cause discomfort when the piece is worn. Also, make sure you reinforce the weakest areas with a decorative motif made of clay (attach it with a little water) in order to prevent breakages.

LACUNA PENDANT

Materials:
- PMC3 5g.
- Basic metal clay kit.
- Mini tube cutters (ferrules) in assorted sizes.
- Needle tool (see Basic Techniques).
- Basic firing kit.
- Steel block and hammer.
- 5mm x 10mm sterling silver bail or one open jump ring 4.5mm, 21 gauge (approx. 0.76mm).
- Chain (18 inch long).

Making the pendant

1. Roll a clay sheet 3 depth cards thick (0.75mm).

2. Rotate the work mat so the longest part of the clay is horizontal.

3. Place the number 3 depth cards at either side of the clay.

4. Rest the number 1 (ace) card across the clay and the number 3 depth cards.

5. Run the upright needle tool along the edge of the 1 card to cut a straight line 30mm long.

6. 6mm below the previous one, make a parallel cut.

7. Trim the ends to form a 30mm long by 6mm wide rectangle.

8. Cut out a small hole near one of the shorter edges (approximately 2mm away from the edge), for the bail.

9. Create a pattern with the mini cutters.

10. Dry thoroughly, and carefully refine the edges if needed.

11. Fire for two minutes (see Basic Techniques).

12. Wire brush, burnish and polish.

13. Use Liver of Sulphur (LOS) patina if desired (see A Touch of Colour).

14. Push open the jump ring (or bail ring). Insert through the hole in the pendant and close the ring (see Basic Techniques).

Design option: for a horizontal bar make a hole on the top corners 2mm from the edge.

Sketch transferred to scratch foam.

Creating a strong frame for a Lacuna design

Some Lacuna designs will require a stronger edge frame in order to keep their structural integrity, particularly if a large amount of material is removed. A simple solution to this design challenge is to incorporate a thicker edge frame as the sheet of clay is rolled out.

To do this, you will need:
- A sketch of your design.
- Tracing paper.
- Sticky tape.
- Scratch foam (very thin sheet of polystyrene).
- Embossing pen.
- Silver clay.
- Basic metal clay kit.
- Acrylic block.

Transfer your design on to the tracing paper. Secure the tracing paper on to the scratch foam with the tape. Carefully trace the design onto the foam with the small ball tip of the embossing pen. Remove the tracing paper and go over the embossed lines once more to deepen the grooves. Do not press too hard or you will create a dimple in the line.

Preparation: In order to have a level surface to support your depth cards/slats and create a good impression of your design, place the depth cards/slats directly on the foam at either side of the design, leaving a little room at either side for the clay to expand. However, if the foam with the design is not large enough to accommodate the depth cards/slats comfortably, get some additional depth cards and place them next to the foam to match the foam's thickness.

To roll the clay sheet:

1. Roll the clay 1.25mm thick (5 depth cards/slats) on a separate work mat.

2. Lift the sheet of clay and carefully place it over the design on the foam, ensuring the design is completely covered.

3. Cover the clay with a work mat.

4. Place 4 depth cards (1mm) at either side of the clay and then use the acrylic block to firmly press the clay down into the design, making sure the acrylic block rests on the depth cards.

5. Remove the acrylic block and depth slats.

6. Cover the clay with a work mat and flip it over, so the foam is on top.

7. Carefully separate the foam from the clay. You should have a clean print of your design.

8. With the tip of a craft knife slowly cut around the design, making sure not to 'drag' the clay (you can clean the edges once the clay is dry).

Now that you have the frame, you can proceed to create the Lacuna gaps using different-sized cutters, either randomly or in an organised pattern. To create pits and dimples use the different-sized balls of the embossing pen, and the needle tool or craft knife to create slashes and small gaps.

CHAPTER EIGHT

A Touch of Colour

A TOUCH OF COLOUR will add interest to your jewellery designs. This can be done using patinas like Liver of Sulphur (LOS), an oxidising solution (Black Magic) or with plain glass seed beads (not silver-lined or galvanised). Although there are additional colouring methods, they require greater technical knowledge and special equipment, therefore we will concentrate on the more accessible and easy to use.

'PLIQUE-A-JOUR' HEART PENDANT

Glass seed beads in blues, greens, purple and black colours make ideal decorative elements (other colours do not survive the heating process). These beads are locked in place as the clay shrinks during the firing process, creating a 'plique-a-jour' effect as light passes through the glass (reminiscent of stained glass).

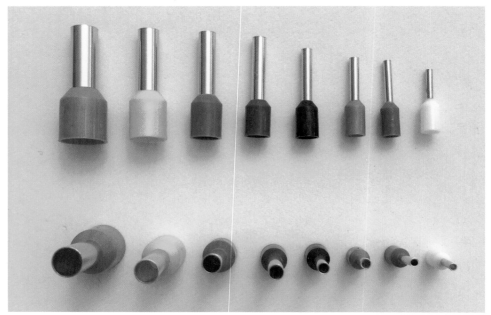

For these projects you will need:

- PMC3 16g.
- Basic metal clay kit.
- Miyuki glass seed beads 11/0 (not silver-lined or galvanised). Light blue, dark blue, green and purple work best.
- Mini tube cutters in assorted sizes.
- A pin (or piece of wire, needle).
- 4cm heart template or cutter.
- Basic firing kit.
- Finishing kit.
- 15mm sterling silver ring bail.
- Flat-nose pliers and chain-nose pliers.

Making the pendant

1. First, place a seed bead flat on a level surface with the hole running parallel to the surface.

2. Find a tube cutter that just fits over the seed bead (if the bead gets stuck inside the tube, use the pin, a piece of wire or a needle to dislodge it).

3. Set the tube aside, ready to use.

4. Roll a sheet of clay 0.75mm thick (3 depth cards).

5. Cut out a heart shape either with the cutter, or with the template and a needle tool (remembering to keep the needle tool upright).

6. With the tube cutter make a hole 2mm below the 'v' at the top of the heart (this is the opening for the bail).

7. Now work your way down from that hole to cut out three more holes, evenly spaced. Do not make the openings too close to each other.

8. Fill each hole with a different coloured seed bead (do not place a seed bead in the hole for the bail!).

9. Place each seed bead above the opening, with the hole in the seed bead running flat, and gently push the bead all the way in.

10. Next, create a row of holes at either side of the first line. Start roughly midway between seed beads (see photo on opposite page).

11. Fill each opening with a different coloured seed bead. Continue creating rows towards the edges, but being careful to preserve at least 2mm at the edge.

12. Allow the piece to dry. As it dries, the shrinking will lock the seed beads in place.

13. Once dried, carefully refine the edges with a nail file. Make sure the seed beads are free from dust and clay residue, otherwise the silver will stain the glass permanently. If a bead comes loose, dampen the hole by adding a drop of water, wait a few seconds and then reposition the bead.

14. Fire for two minutes as normal. Move the flame evenly over the clay and beads. Do not quench in water. Instead allow the piece to cool slowly so as not to shatter the glass. Please note that the glass seed beads will glow red as you fire the clay. This is normal and they will go back to their original colour as they gradually cool down.

15. Once the piece has cooled down completely, wire brush. Then use a micro polishing pad to bring a little sheen over the top and bottom surfaces.

16. Bring the edges to a mirror finish with an agate burnisher.

17. To attach the bail, carefully push the ring open. Insert the bail into the pendant's hole, ensuring the opening of the ring ends are at the back of the pendant. Close the bail's ring. If needed, adjust with the chain-nose pliers.

ADDING COLOUR USING PATINAS

Liver of Sulphur (LOS) is the most commonly used patina. It adds visual depth and contrast to the silver. LOS comes in three different presentations: dry 'lumps' (which need to be dissolved in water) and liquid or gel (both of which are pre-mixed and contain stabilisers to prolong shelf life). Liquid and gel LOS can be applied directly with a brush (aqua-brushes are ideal for this), or mixed with water.

LOS produces a range of colours depending on the length of time it is in contact with the silver, from soft golden tones, pinks and purples, all the way to deep blue-greens. These colour variations change depending on the water used (from the tap, from a well, or distilled), with the water's temperature (lukewarm or hot, but NEVER boiling as this will render the solution ineffective) and with the strength of the solution. Note that a weak solution yields very pale colours, but a strong solution can act too fast, and is difficult to control.

It is important to follow the manufacturer's instructions, to work in a well-ventilated room and to protect clothing and surfaces.

An oxidising solution, also known as Black Magic, produces a strong black patina as soon as it comes in contact with the silver. However, the excess patina can be easily removed from the high points of the silver with a micro-polishing pad. Oxidising solution is ideal to create a dramatic contrast, and is particularly good when working with deeper textures.

An aqua-brush filled with oxidising solution (make sure you label the brush) is ideal, as it provides great control when applying the solution and makes it easy to use.

Again, it is important to follow the manufacturer's instructions, to work in a well-ventilated room and to protect clothing and surfaces.

After application, both Liver of Sulphur and oxidising solution need to be neutralised by rinsing the piece in a simple solution of half a teaspoon of bicarbonate of soda dissolved in half a cup of water, and then rinsing in clean water. It is advisable to designate three small shallow glass dishes for patina work: one for Liver of Sulphur (LOS), one for neutralising solution (water and bicarbonate), and one with clean water. (I have mine on an oven tray, ready to use.)

The patina sequence:

1. Burnish your fired silver pieces to a mirror finish (silver clay pieces are slightly porous after firing, so it is better to compact the metal with an agate burnisher).

2. Wash with a drop of washing-up liquid to remove any oils and dry with a clean paper towel.

3. Hold the piece with tweezers, or use a

piece of wire to suspend it if using diluted LOS.

4. Apply the patina, either by immersion or using a brush, until satisfied with colour.

5. Dip in bicarbonate and water (half a teaspoon in half a cup of water) solution for a few seconds, and then rinse in clean water.

6. Dry with a clean paper towel.

7. Use a micro polishing pad or a soft polishing cloth to remove the excess patina that sits on the top surface. The patina sitting in the crevices and recesses will remain in place.

Permanent marker pens (medium and fine tips)

These pens enable you to darken the silver recesses and thus avoid using chemical patinas. Simply scribble over the recessed surface, then remove the excess with a micro polishing pad.

CHAPTER NINE

Found Textures

TEXTURES CAN BE found everywhere, and the malleable properties of metal clay offer endless possibilities for capturing these interesting textures and patterns. From the intricate pattern of a netting bag (often used for fruit), to the markings created by an old toothbrush or even a loved one's fingerprint.

In this project you will learn how to incorporate found textures and how to create a pair of contemporary earrings.

Materials:
- Basic metal clay kit.
- PMC3 16g.
- An old toothbrush.
- Circle cutter (15mm diameter), or circle template and needle tool.
- Thin straw or tube ferrules.
- Basic firing kit.
- Oxidising solution (Black Magic), Liver of Sulphur (LOS) or permanent marker.
- Agate burnisher.
- Micro-polishing pads.

Texturing and shaping the clay:

1. Apply a drop of olive oil onto the bristles of the toothbrush and gently work the oil into the brush (this will prevent sticking).

2. Roll a metal clay sheet three cards thick (0.75mm).

3. Gently stipple the surface on one half of the rolled out clay (do not push all the way down as this will weaken the piece). Use a card to mask part of the clay if you would like to have a straight line dividing the textured area.

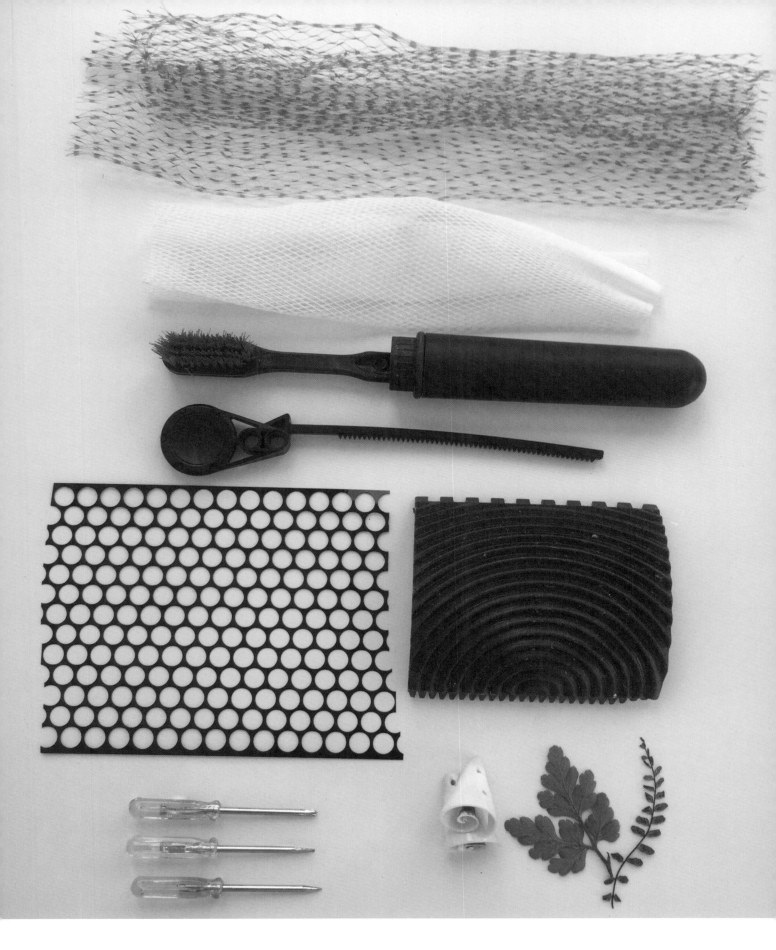

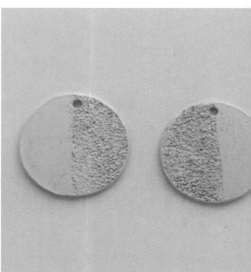

4. Use the circle cutter or the circle template as a viewfinder to select the most attractive area to use, half textured and half plain works best, but you have creative choice.

5. Place the circle cutter on the clay and gently press into the clay. 'Jiggle' the cutter a little to free the cut out shape. Remove the excess clay and store it in the packet. If using a circle template, let it rest on the depth cards at either side of the clay. Use the needle tool in an upright position (90 degrees to the clay) and trace around the circle. Please note that it is very important to keep the needle tool upright in order to get a consistent edge. If the tool is slanted you will get uneven angled edges that will require sorting out later.

6. Decide the orientation of your piece (vertical, horizontal or diagonal texture line).

7. Make a small hole 2mm below the edge at the top of the design using the thin straw or small tube ferrule.

8. Allow the circle to dry. Do not worry about any residue left along the edges, you'll be able to refine them once the circle has completely dried.

9. Repeat steps 1 to 8. If you would like to have a slightly larger pendant then use a larger shaped cutter/template.

10. Once the circles are dry, gently run your finger along the edge of each circle to loosen any residue/blemish. If your pieces need further refinement you can use a nail file to smooth the edge, or you can run a wet wipe along the edge to heal any imperfection.

11. Fire each piece for two minutes.

12. Quench the pieces and wire brush them to a satin finish.

13. Polish the edges and the untextured areas with the agate burnisher, to bring them to a mirror finish. You can either burnish the untextured half to a high polish or leave it with a satin finish. If the orientation of your design is vertical, ensure the earrings are a mirror image (textured area is either in the centre for both earrings, or on the outside).

14. Use oxidising solution, Liver of Sulphur or permanent marker pen to darken the textured area following the manufacturer's instructions.

15. Remove the patina excess with a polishing cloth, or micro polishing pad.

16. Bring to a sheen with a polishing cloth.

Design options: A simple way to add interest to a piece is by the use of wire extensions (pendulums). Suspending the textured discs on a wire pendulum adds movement to piece, giving it more presence. Please see Versatile Rods chapter for instructions on how to make the pendulums.

FINGERPRINT JEWELLERY

Fingerprint jewellery makes a great keepsake. There are endless design options, but the starting point is the same for all: a fingerprint.

The most effective way of harvesting a print is to press directly onto the clay, but the print area must not be too shallow, which can occur if too much pressure is applied on the spot. In order to avoid this, follow these steps:

1. Roll the clay four cards thick (1mm).

2. Gently but firmly press a finger onto the clay. Adult's prints are very clear, so any finger will yield a good impression. Young children's fingerprints are very faint, so thumb prints are a better option and, for a baby, the big toe works well. Rather than letting children press into the clay (they can push too hard), just bring the rolled out clay on a firm surface to the child's finger or toe, gently hold their hand or foot to prevent wriggling, and press the clay to harvest the print.

3. Once the print is clear, cut the clay to the desired shape. Make a hole for the bail, then allow to dry.

4. Refine and fire as usual.

5. To bring out the fingerprint and enhance the contrast of its ridges, apply some patina directly on the print, let it sit for a few seconds and then gently remove the excess with a polishing cloth.

Please note that if a name is going to accompany the print, this should be done after the print has been obtained. If using mini-stamps, use while the clay is fresh. However, if the name is going to be etched with a stylus, wait until the clay has dried completely.

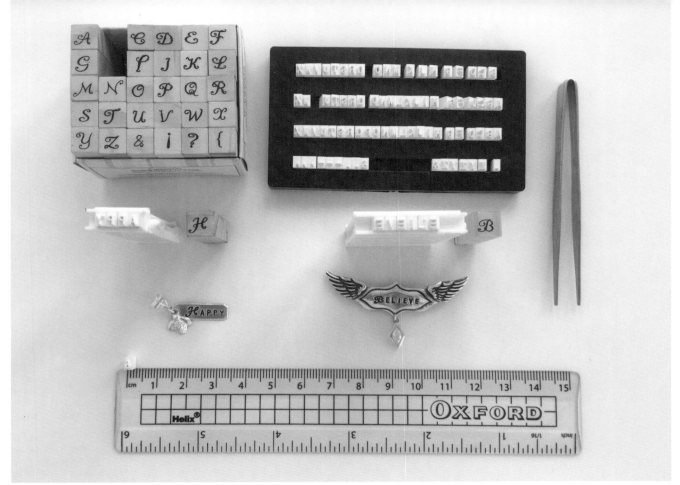

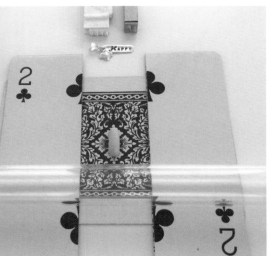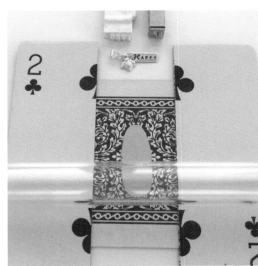

CHAPTER TEN

From Nature

MAKING JEWELLERY WITH LEAVES, SMALL PLANTS AND FLOWERS

Jewellery that captures the beauty and delicate nature of small flowers and plants is always popular. This can be achieved by taking a direct impression of a favourite plant, a petal from a wedding bouquet, a small flower, a skeleton leaf, or by creating reusable silicone moulds.

LEAF PENDANT

Materials:
- Basic metal clay kit.
- PMC3 5g.
- Two oval 22 gauge open jump rings 4.3mm x 3.5mm.
- 5cm of 18 gauge (1.02mm) sterling silver wire.
- Flush cutters.
- Round-nose pliers.
- Leaf or skeleton leaf (used in crafts).
- 15mm leaf-shaped cutter or leaf template (alternatively use a geometric shape).
- 10mm circle cutter or template.
- Small tube cutters (ferrule) or thin straw.
- Basic firing kit.
- Agate burnisher.

Forming the pendant:

1. Roll a metal clay sheet 3 depth cards thick (0.75mm). If using a leaf with deep veins increase to 4 cards.

2. Remove the number 3 depth cards and replace with number 2 depth cards (0.50mm).

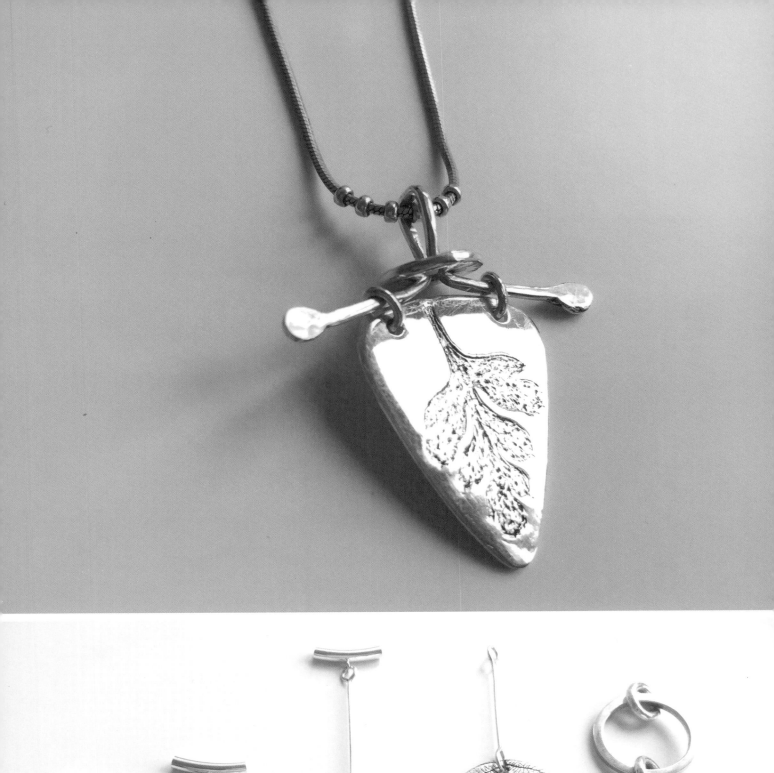

3. Place the leaf on top of the metal clay sheet. Make sure the pronounced central ridge is in contact with the clay and the tip of the leaf points towards you (the stalk should point away from you).

4. Press the leaf onto the clay with a gentle rolling motion, ensuring the roller stays in contact with the cards/slats. To prevent an uneven or fuzzy print, roll from the centre of the leaf up, then from the centre down and finally over the entire leaf.

5. With the needle tool, gently and carefully peel off the leaf by lifting the stalk and pulling the leaf towards you.

6. Place the leaf-shaped cutter (or stencil) with the pointed end towards you (the central vein should be centred). Gently press the shaped cutter into the clay, and jiggle it a little to free the cut out shape. If you are using a template, use the needle tool to cut the shape out. If the template's shape is too big, you can trim to a suitable size. Remove the excess clay and store it in the packet.

7. Make two small holes 2mm from the top of the pendant (the broad end), using the straw/tube. Make sure the holes are at either side of the leaf's central vein, approximately 1cm apart. Please note, when making a pendant with a single bail hole, make sure the hole lines up with the central vein (see photos on previous page).

8. Allow the leaf to dry. Do not worry about any residue left along the edges, you'll be able to refine them once the shape has completely dried.

9. Once the shape is dry, gently run your finger along the edge to loosen any residue/blemish. If your piece needs further refinement you can use a nail file to smooth the edge, or you can run a wet wipe along the edge to heal any imperfection.

10. Fire the piece for two minutes if it is small or for three minutes if it is large.

11. Quench (cool down) the piece and wire brush to a satin finish.

12. Polish with the agate burnisher to a mirror finish. The leaf print recess will remain matt.

13. Apply patina to the leaf print (LOS, oxidising solution or permanent marker).

14. Polish off excess patina.

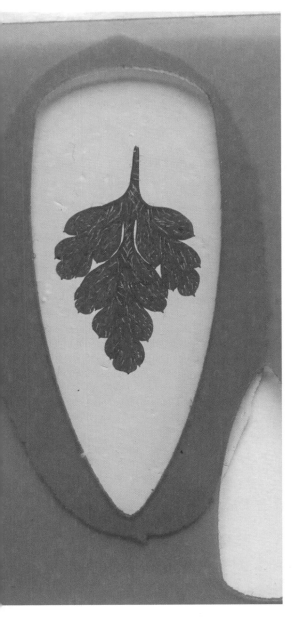
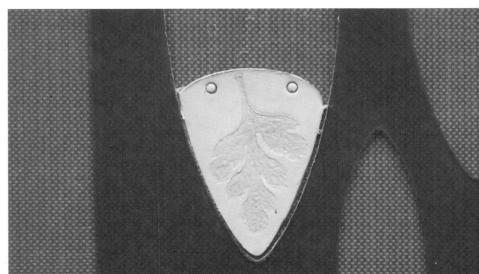

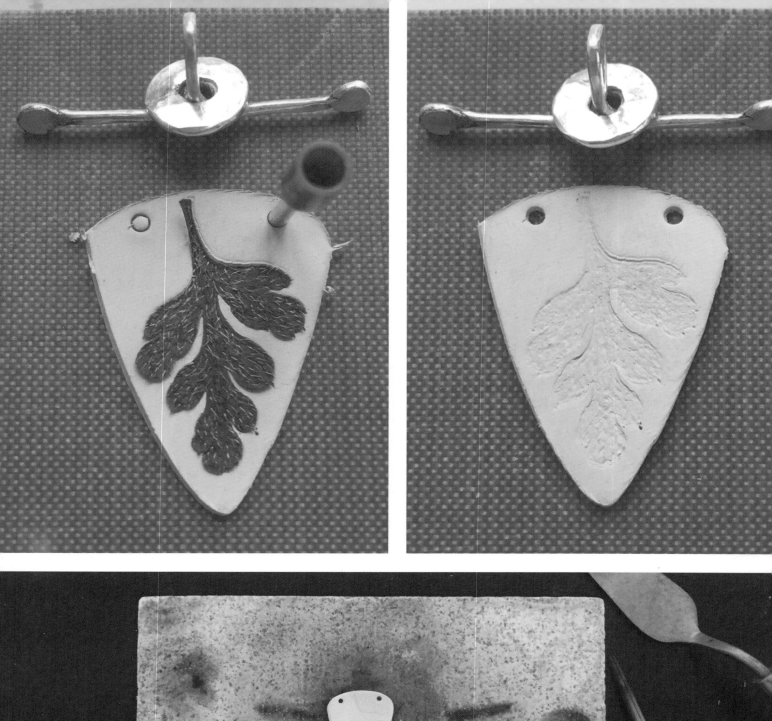
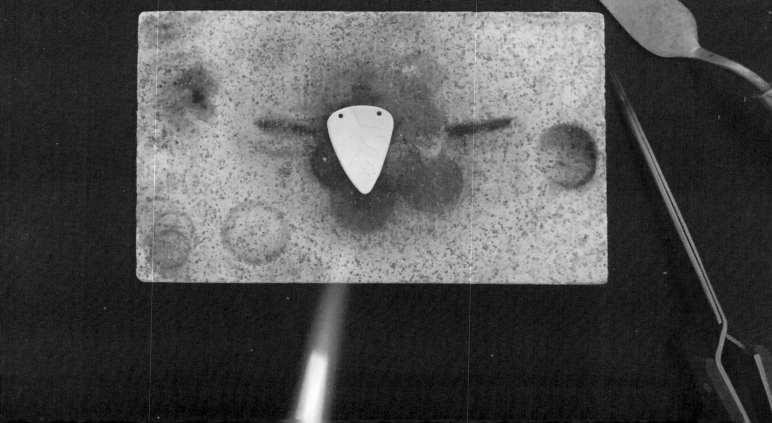

When making a piece with a complete leaf print, you have a couple of finishing options:

A. Burnish one half of the leaf to a high polish, and leave the other half with a satin finish. If making earrings, ensure they are placed side by side and polish the outer side only and leave the inner sections satin.

B. Burnish the entire piece to a mirror finish (note that some texture definition is lost with this finish).

Making the bail:

1. Roll out a clay sheet 3 depth cards (0.75mm) thick.

2. Cut a circle 10mm in diameter.

3. Cut a 3mm hole in the centre of the circle with a small tube cutter (ferrule) to form a small ring.

4. Refine, fire, polish and hammer finish the small ring. Set aside.

5. On the tip of the round-nose pliers bend the 5cm of wire in half to form an upside down 'U' shape (see pictures overleaf).

6. Feed the wire ends through the small ring's hole.

7. Bring the ring up close to the bend (3–5mm), then push apart the wire's ends. This will form a bail.

8. Ball both ends of the wire (see Basic Techniques chapter). Do not make large balls. Please note: you will need to repolish the pieces, but it will be quicker.

9. Place the balled wire on the steel block and gently hammer the balls to flatten them, using the flat side of the chasing hammer to do so.

10. Gently tap the rest of the wire to work harden it.

11. Polish and burnish. If the fire-scale (the dark layer that forms when sterling silver is heated) persists, place the wire in a small dish and cover the piece with lemon juice and add 1/4 teaspoon of salt. Let it sit there for fifteen minutes. Then scrub with the toothbrush and rinse.

12 Finally, join the bail and pendant with the jump rings. Open the jump rings (see Basic Techniques chapter), insert the pendant and close the jump rings.

13. Adjust the wire to accommodate the pendant. The slack on

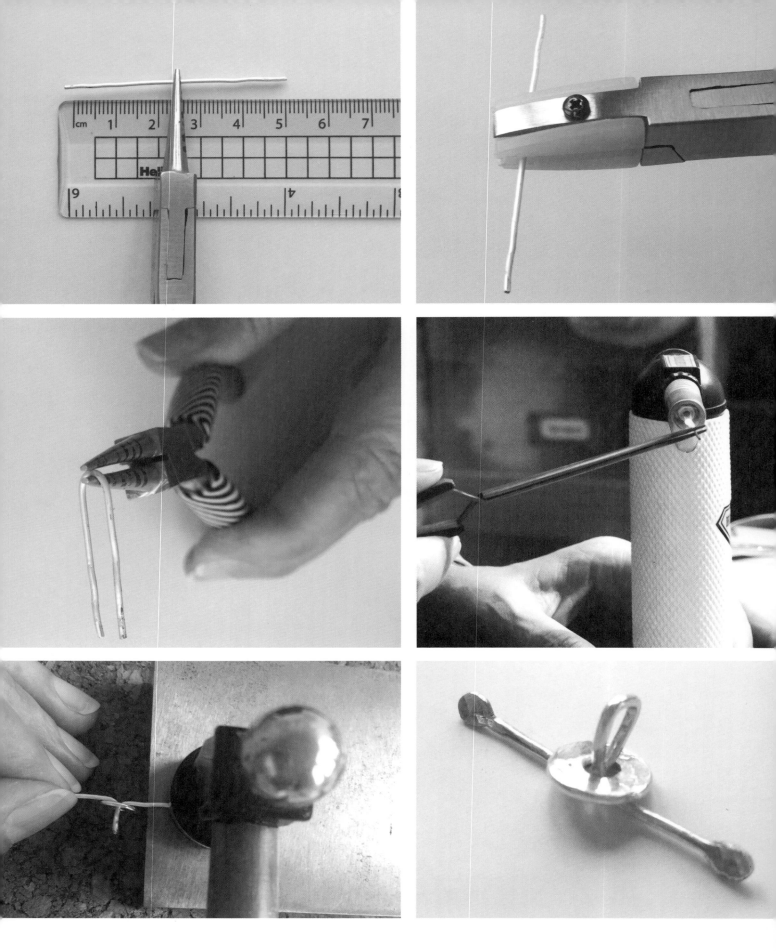

the jump rings in relation to the pendant should be enough to allow free movement, but not so much that the jump rings slide off the wire completely. The flat balls (paddles) should stop this from happening.

MAKING AND USING MOULDS

Capturing the beauty and delicate nature of small flowers and plants into reusable silicone moulds is easy.

I use Pëbëo silicone-Siligum, a two-part moulding compound, to make these simple moulds.:

1. Just mix equal parts of the moulding compound into an even colour putty (for a small flower or fern, a chickpea-sized ball from each of the tubs will be enough).

2. For a small leaf or fern mould, place a small amount of the mixed moulding compound on to a playing card or a Teflon mat, and roll to 4 depth cards thick (1mm).

3. Remove the number 4 depth cards and replace with the number 3 depth cards to reduce to 0.75mm, place the plant material on top of the compound (ensure the most prominent ridges are in contact with the silicone), and gently roll over the plant material.

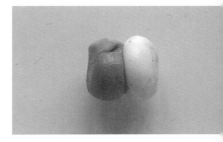

4. Allow to cure undisturbed (usually takes 5–10 minutes).

5. Once the silicone has set, carefully take the plant material off. You should now have a clear print of the plant sample ready to use.

6. For larger/deeper plant samples like a daisy, the silicone compound must be rolled out thicker.

HOW TO USE FLAT MOULDS

1. Find depth cards equal to the thickness of the silicone mould.

2. Roll a sheet of clay 5 cards thick (1.25mm).

3. Remove the number 5 depth cards and replace with number 3 depth cards (0.75mm) plus the cards the same thickness as the mould (from 1 above).

4. Place the silicone mould over the rolled out clay and press down with the acrylic block.

5. Gently separate the clay from the mould. The plant imprint should be clear and clean.

6. Cut the clay to the desired shape. Remember to make a hole for the findings

7. Allow to dry, then refine the edges.

8. Fire and polish as normal.

9. Use patina to highlight the pattern.

Please note: if you prefer to press the clay over the silicone mould, you first need to match the thickness of the mould with the depth cards/slats (as in 1 above). Then place the number 3 cards over the ones matching the mould. Put a pinch of clay over the mould and press.

HOW TO WORK WITH CONCAVE MOULDS

1. If using small shells (or concave forms), make a small silicone ball and then press the shell into it.

2. Allow the silicone to cure and then remove the shell.

3. Press a small amount of clay inside the mould and wipe off the excess. Note that the same shell used to create the mould can also be pressed into the clay if you wish to texture it from both sides.

4. If needed, carefully make a hole with a needle tool whilst the clay is fresh, or with a small hand drill if the clay has dried.

5. Allow to dry in the mould and then remove it.

6. Refine, fire and polish as usual.

CHAPTER ELEVEN

Versatile Rods

A SIMPLE WAY TO add interest and movement to a piece is by including wire rods in the design. A rod is simply a length of wire, either plain or embellished. Wire rods are simple to make, or can be purchased ready-made as either headpins or eyepins. They can be reshaped and altered by gentle hammering, or by splaying the wire's end to form paddles (as in the previous project). Rods can also be decorated with beads and tubes, or used in combination with other silver pieces to create original components.

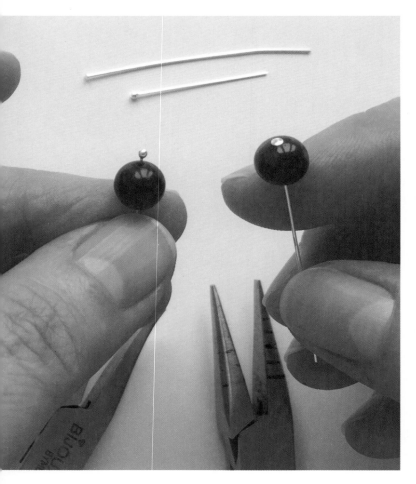

A wire rod with a flat end, or a ball, is called a headpin, and is used to attach embellishments like pearls or beads. Headpins can also be fashioned into earring hooks. Rods with a simple loop at one end are eyepins, and with a loop at both ends become connectors, or a pendulum, depending on the use. A loop with a wraparound end is a wrapped loop. These can have a traditional uniform wrap, like a coil, or a 'knotted' random wrap to complement an organic design. Wire wrapped loops are ideal to securely attach connectors and decorative elements, and to make custom bails. The possibilities are endless!

In this chapter we will create a pair of hammered earrings made with wire rods, and also explore how to make pendulums, connectors and headpins. But we will first cover a few wire essentials.

WIRE ESSENTIALS

As noted earlier, **wire gauge** refers to the thickness of the wire. The higher the gauge number, the thinner the wire. When the measurements are in inches or millimetres, the higher the number the thicker the wire.

Temper refers to the hardness of the wire: dead-soft, half-hard and full-hard. It ranges from very pliable to very stiff.

Annealing is heating a metal to make it more workable and flexible. Full-hard wire can be annealed with a blowtorch and will become dead soft. You can do this by forming a loose coil, placing it on a firebrick and gently heating the wire until it reaches the pale salmon colour, and then allowing it to cool naturally or quenching it in water.

Work-hardening. All wire hardens as you manipulate it; this is called work-hardening. Work-hardened pieces are stronger and hold their shape better. To work-harden wire after it has been shaped, place it on a steel block and gently tap the wire with a nylon hammer.

HAMMERED ROD EARRINGS

You will need:
- Safety goggles.
- Round concave pliers.
- Chain-nose pliers.
- Flat-nose nylon jaw pliers.
- Flush cutters.
- 1mm/18 gauge sterling silver wire, or ready-made eyepins (go straight to texturing if using eyepins).
- 1-inch chasing hammer, steel block and cork mat.
- Pair of sterling silver 3/4 hoops.

The process to make the rod earrings includes a number of steps: straightening the wire, forming the loop (creating eyepins), texturing and, finally, assembling the earring.

Straightening the wire
Wire often bends or kinks, but getting it back to shape is easy! Firmly grab one end of the wire with the chain-nose pliers and run the flat-nose nylon jaw pliers along the wire. Repeat if necessary.

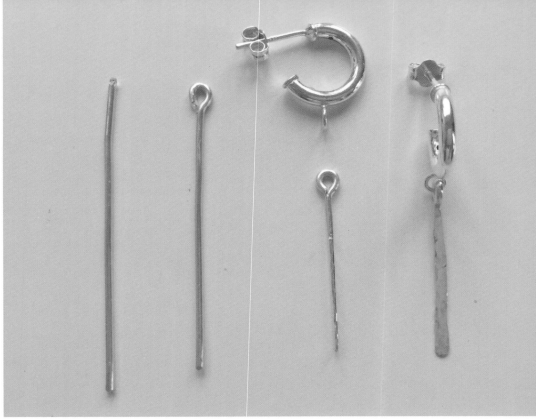

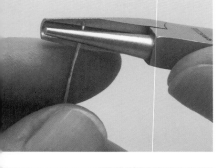

Forming the wires: simple loop

With a permanent marker pen, make a mark across the nose of the round concave pliers, approximately 3mm from the tip of the pliers. This will ensure you form consistent loops (see Lacuna chapter).

Making a simple loop with round concave pliers

1. Cut two equal lengths of wire 3cm long with the flush cutters.

2. Hold the tip of one wire with the round-nose pliers, making sure the wire lines up with 3mm mark.

3. Rotate the pliers fully until you meet the wire to form a loop (at this stage it will look like a 'P').

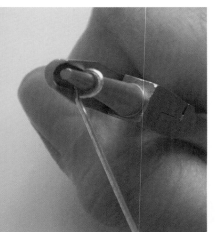

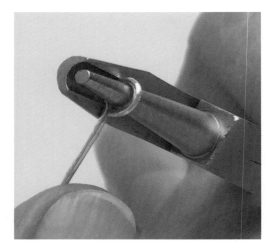

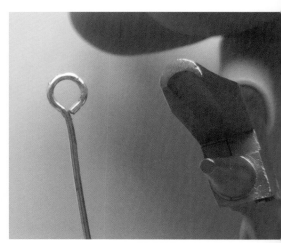

4. Rotate the wire on the nose of the pliers until the long end of the wire rests on the edge of the concave jaw.

5. Gently push the wire a little against the concave edge to centre the stem (the loop will look now like a balloon or a lollipop).

6. Repeat process for second wire.

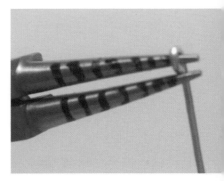

Making a simple loop with round-nose pliers (instead of using concave pliers)

1. Cut two equal lengths of wire 3cm long with the flush cutters.

2. Hold the tip of one wire with the round-nose pliers, making sure the wire lines up with the mark.

3. Rotate the pliers fully until you meet the wire to form a loop (at this stage it will look like a 'P'). Remove the pliers.

4. Insert one tip of the pliers into the loop so you can grasp the long side of the wire, directly across from the loop's opening (the point where the wire's tip meets the long side of the wire).

5. Make a sharp 45-degree bend towards the long side of the wire. This will centre the loop over the length of wire and it will now look like a balloon or a lollipop.

6. Repeat process for second wire.

Texturing the wire

1. Place the wire on a steel block. Hold in place by the loop, making sure the loop overhangs perpendicular to the surface of the block. The wire must be positioned so the loop's join is below, so that there is a continuous line.

2. With the ball end of the chasing hammer, gently tap the length of the wire, starting from the end and working your way up towards the loop area. As the wire flattens, concentrate the blows towards the end of the wire; this will create a taper in that area.

3. Straighten the wire with flat-nose pliers.

4. Burnish the wire (front, back and edges) with an agate burnisher.

You now have the completed rods for the earrings.

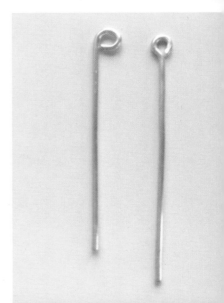

Making paddle ends (design option)

We can make the piece more interesting by adding paddle ends to the wire. This needs to be done before the wire is cut and the loops are made, and the process is as follows:

1. With a torch, ball the ends of the wire (see Basic Techniques).

2. Cut wire in half.

3. Make a loop on the straight end of the wire (follow the instructions above).

4. Place the wire on a steel block. Hold in place by the loop, making sure the loop overhangs perpendicular to the surface of the block. The wire must be positioned so the loop's join is below, so that there is a continuous line.

5. With the ball head of the chasing hammer, gently tap the balled wire to form paddles. As the balls flatten, concentrate the blows towards the ends.

6. File and burnish the wire's ends smooth. If necessary, pickle the wire in lemon juice and a pinch of salt, to remove the darkening on the balls.

7. Burnish the wire (front, back and edges) with agate burnisher.

Making the earrings
1. Push open the loop of the wire rod (eyepin).

2. Insert it into the small ring of the earring hoop (the loop's opening should be facing away from the front of the earring hoop).

3. Carefully close the loop.

You have now completed the rod earrings.

How to make wire rod pendulums and connectors
Pendulums and connectors add a new dimension to your pieces. Both add length and movement. In addition, they can be embellished with beads or pearls and be joined to form bespoke chains.

You will need:
• Safety goggles.
• Round concave pliers.
• Flush cutters.
• 10cm of sterling wire 18 gauge wire (1mm).

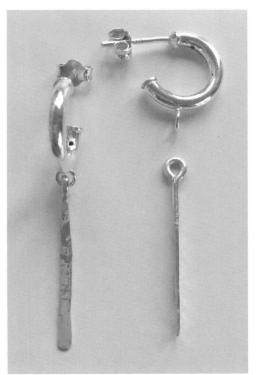

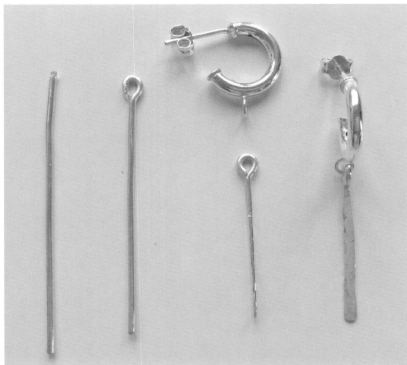

Top left: Hammered rod earrings before and after completion.

Top right: The different stages of making a rod earring.

Left: Wire connectors attached to decorative connectors to form a necklace.

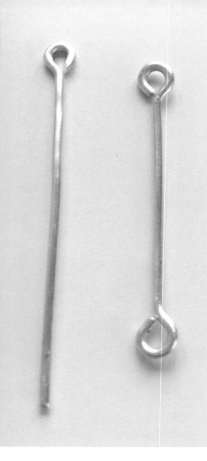

Making a bail pendulum

1. Follow the instructions for making a simple loop with round concave pliers.

2. Repeat process at opposite end (the loops should be curling towards each other).

Making pendulums for earrings

1. For the first loop, the steps are the same as above,

2. Before forming the second loop at the opposite end, turn the wire 90 degrees. Then make the loop as before (hold the first loop between your index finger and thumb of one hand, and form the other loop by holding the pliers horizontally).

3. The second loop should be smaller than the first, which will be attached to the earring hoop. To make the smaller loop, all you need to do is line up the wire with the tip of the round concave pliers and make the loop as before.

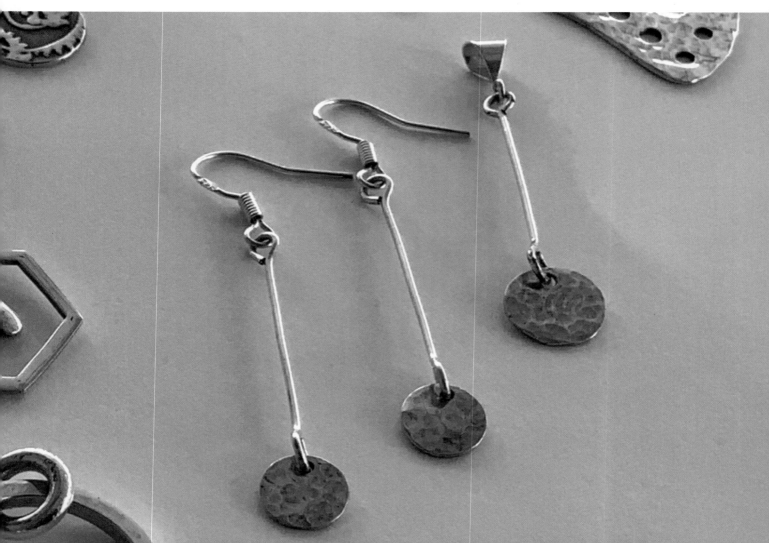

Attaching decorative elements to pendulums

1. To attach the decorative element to the pendulum, open the large loop by pushing past the long side of the wire.

2. Insert the decorative element (patterned side goes first), then close. The loop's opening should be on the reverse side of the decorative element.

3. Follow the same procedure to attach an earring hook to the other end of the pendulum to complete the earrings.

Forming wrapped loops with round concave pliers

Wrapped loops are used to attach components (dangles, beads, connectors, etc.). Certain pieces also require additional strength. A simple loop made from high-gauge wire can become undone if pulled, but it can be made more secure by extending the wire and wrapping it around the base of the loop. Uniform wrapped loops are discreet, but might not suit a particular design, whilst organic wrapped loops beautifully complement nature themed pieces and ethnic styles.

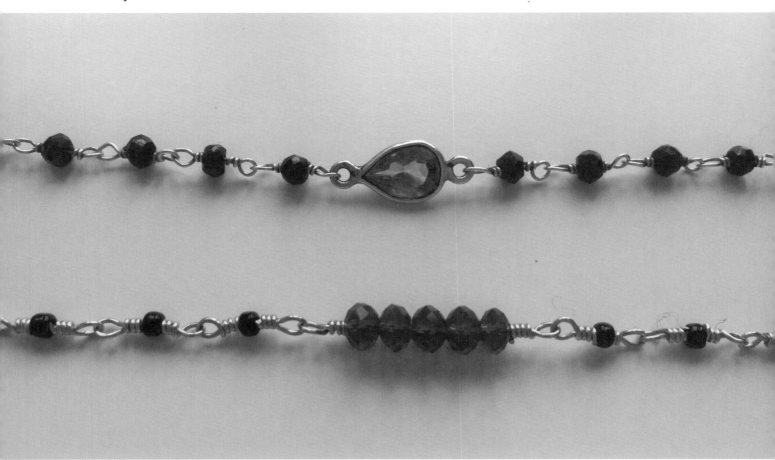

Uniform wraps for bead dangles

You will need:
- Safety goggles.
- Two 3cm long ball headpins.
- Two 5mm semi-precious beads.
- 3/4 hoop earrings.
- Round concave pliers.
- Bent-nose pliers.
- Flush cutters.

1. Insert one ball headpin into each bead. Push the bead until it is flush with the ball.

2. Hold the bead in place by placing the tip of the round concave pliers flush with the bead. The concave jaw should be at the bottom and the round jaw on top.

3. Push bead against the edge of the concave jaw a little.

4. Now bring the wire all the way around the round jaw until it meets the headpin again. You should have a loop which is open at the base.

5. Introduce the long end of the headpin into the small ring of the 3/4 hoop earring.

6. Hold the loop with the bent-nose pliers and wrap the long end around the base of the loop in a neat even coil.

7. With the flush cutters trim the excess wire.

8. Adjust the loop if necessary.

9. Repeat 1 to 8 with the second earring.

Forming wrapped loops with round-nose pliers (alternative to round concave pliers)

1. Insert one-ball headpins into each bead. Push the bead until is flush with the ball.

2. Hold the bead in place by placing the tip of the bent-nose pliers flush with the bead.

3. Gently bend the wire to form a 90-degree angle.

4. Grasp the wire with the round-nose pliers where the wire bends; the nose of the pliers should be vertical, in line with the wire.

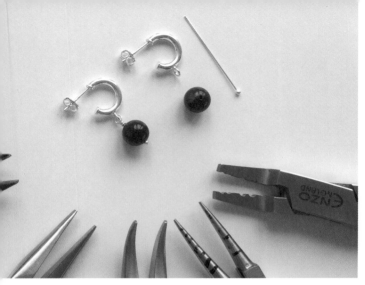

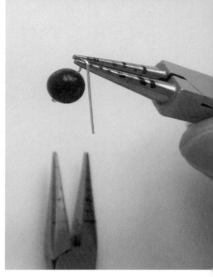

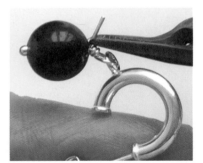

5. Pull the long wire over the top of the round-nose pliers to form a loop and wrap around the base of the loop two or three times. Make sure the wire is taut and that each turn sits next to the previous one, so the wire coil is uniform. If the coils are spread out, use the bent-nose pliers to bring them together.

6. Snip excess wire if necessary with the flush cutters.

7. Use chain-nose pliers to tuck away the tail end of the coil.

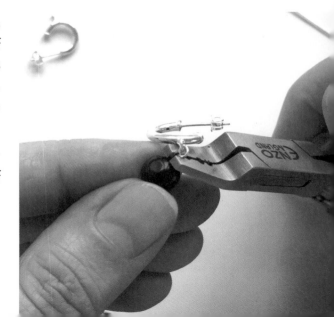

Organic wrap loops

Organic wrap loops need longer wire in order to form a loop and to randomly wrap around the base of the loop.

1. Follow the instructions for making a loop with round concave pliers. You should have an extra-long piece of wire at a 90-degree angle at the base of the open loop.

2. Introduce the long end of the headpin into the small ring of the 3/4 hoop earring.

3. Hold the loop with the bent-nose pliers and randomly wrap the long end around the base of the loop. This will make the wire look 'knotted'.

4. With the flush cutters snip excess wire if necessary.

5. Use chain-nose pliers to tuck away the tail end of the coil.

MAKING HEADPINS AND EARRING HOOKS

You will need:
- Safety goggles, apron and fire extinguisher.
- 10cm of sterling silver wire 0.8mm/20 gauge.
- Insulated reverse-action tweezers.
- Blowtorch and baking tray.
- Glass dish with water.
- Pencil.
- Steel block and nylon hammer.
- Wire rounder tool.

Headpin

1. Safety first: Protect your eyes, tie your hair back (if applicable) and avoid loose clothing.

2. Ball both ends of the wire with the blowtorch as in previous projects (see From Nature).

3. Once you have two pleasing small ball ends, quench the wire into the water dish.

4. Cut the wire in half.

5. With the wire rounder tool smooth the ends.

Forming earring hooks

The process to form earring hooks is the same for wires with a simple

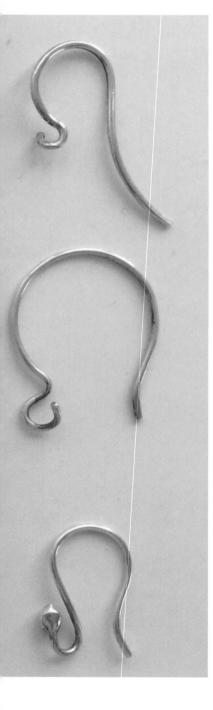

loop (eyepin) and ball headpin. You will need either two 20 gauge (0.8mm) sterling silver eyepins, or two ball headpins.

Using headpins:

1. Hold the headpin by the neck of the ball with the tip of the chain-nose pliers.

2. Bend the neck of the ball so it forms a small 'U' shape. Repeat with second headpin.

3. Place both headpins together on top of the pencil at a 90-degree angle, and bend down to form a hook.

4. Keep the wires on the pencil. Hold the tip of wires with the chain-nose pliers, 2mm in, and bend up a little.

5. Place the hooks on the steel block and gently tap with nylon hammer to work-harden the bend.

6. Smooth the tips of the wire again with the wire rounder tool. Run your finger over the wire end to check for any rough areas still present, use the nail file if necessary to completely smooth the wires. File in one direction only, working from the edge towards the centre.

Using simple loop wires (eyepins)

1. With the tip of the chain-nose pliers hold one eyepin by the neck of the loop.

2. Bend the wire 90 degrees (the loop should be in line with the wire, not perpendicular to it).

3. Repeat with the second eyepin.

4. Now follow steps 3 to 6 as above.

CHAPTER TWELVE

Seamless Rings and Frames

DECORATIVE SEAMLESS FRAMES and rings can be statement pieces in their own right either by size, numbers or design. They are ideal to frame or showcase another component, and to add simple kinetic movement to a piece.

These frames are not only versatile, but they are also easy to make. In this project we will explore a couple of style options, namely a plain ring and a hexagon frame.

DECORATIVE PLAIN RING

This ring can be worn as a pendant, or can be part of a combination piece.

You will need:
- PMC3 16g.
- Basic metal clay kit.
- Small tube cutters (ferrules).
- Shallow texture plate (optional).
- Geometric template and needle tool (22mm diameter).
- Whiteboard pen.
- Basic firing kit.
- Steel block and 1inch chasing hammer.
- One 8mm diameter x 16 gauge open jump ring (1.3mm), or two for combination pieces.

Forming the ring
1. Roll a clay sheet 5 depth cards thick (1.25mm).
2. Select the desired external size for the ring. Make a mark by it on the template with a whiteboard pen so you remember which it

is. Place the template over the clay, resting on the depth cards. Use the needle tool upright to cut out the outer circle. Remove excess clay.

3. Select a circle three sizes smaller for the inner ring, which will give you a ring 2mm thick. With the whiteboard pen make a mark by the second circle.

4. Centre the geometric template over the clay disc. Use the needle tool upright to cut the inner ring. Keeping the template in place, remove the clay from the centre. The template will hold the clay in place and prevent distortion.

5. Dry thoroughly, and then refine the edges if needed.

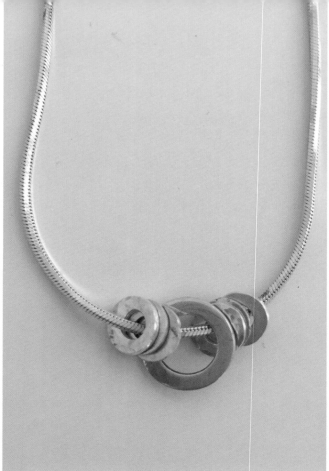

6. Fire for two minutes if the ring is small, or three minutes for a larger ring.

7. Wire brush as usual.

8. Place ring on steel block and gently tap all over with the nylon hammer to work-harden.

9. Burnish and patina as desired.

10. Push open the jump ring. Insert the decorative ring and close the jump ring.

Design options:

A. The ring can be attached to a bail (make sure the bail is in keeping with the size of the ring).

B. Alternatively, two small perforations could be made in the ring before it is fired using the smallest/thinnest tube cutter (ferrule), positioned at '10 past and 10 to', so that the ring can be attached to a chain with jump rings.

C. Another option is to make lateral perforations (suitable for deep rings 2+mm). The perforations are made with a needle, on a fresh clay ring, as follows:

How to make lateral holes in a 2+mm deep ring:

You will need:
- Safety goggles, apron and extinguisher.
- Two headpins 0.4mm or 0.5mm.
- One needle slightly thicker than the headpins.
- Olive oil or Badger Balm.
- Depth cards.
- Smooth round pencil, or cylindrical object small enough to fit inside the ring.
- Basic firing kit.
- Steel block.
- 1-inch chasing hammer.
- A little patience!

1. Follow the instructions 1 to 4 for decorative plain ring.

2. Lubricate the needle with a drop of oil or a small amount of Badger Balm.

3. If your ring is 4 cards deep, place two cards next to the ring (this helps to find the midpoint). Rest the needle on the cards beside the ring and gently push it all the way through. Use the pencil inside the ring to help you preserve its form.

4. Gently release the needle and repeat on the other side of the ring.

5. Allow to dry.

6. Fire, wire brush and burnish as usual.

7. Insert the pins from inside the ring (the heads will rest flat against the inner wall of the ring).

8. Form a small loop with one wrap.

9. Hammer texture the ring after inserting the pins. By inserting the pins first, the gentle hammering will trap the pins in place.

HEXAGONAL FRAME

This frame is ideal to showcase a charm or decorative dangle. It has a tab with an opening to accommodate both a bail and a charm or dangle.

You will need:
- PMC3 5g.

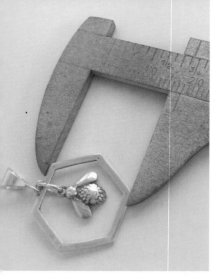

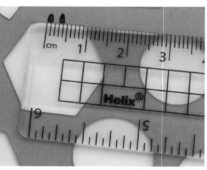

- Basic Tool Kit.
- 2mm tube cutter (ferrules).
- Geometric template and needle tool.
- Whiteboard pen.
- Firing kit.
- Steel block and hammer.
- Small bail 5mm x 8mm (ring included).
- One 4.3mm x 3.5 x 22 gauge (0.64mm) oval open jump ring.
- Small charm or decorative dangle.

Preparation:

1. Select the desired size for your hexagon (the one shown is 18mm x 21mm x 1mm and 2 cards deep). Find the centre of one of the sides. With the whiteboard pen make a mark 3mm at either side of the centre (this will create a 6mm gap). You now have a start and a stop cutting mark.

2. Grab the tube cutter with the chain-nose pliers and gently press to create a slightly oval shape.

3. Roll a clay sheet 2 depth cards thick (0.5mm). For a hammered finish, roll the clay to 3 depth cards thick (0.75mm).

4. Place the geometric template over the clay, resting on the depth cards. Use the needle tool upright to cut out the outer hexagon. Remember to start and stop at the marked points.

5. Lift the geometric template. With the needle tool, make two 5mm long, parallel cuts starting from the start-stop marks and at 90 degrees to the hexagon. Cut away from the hexagon to form a tab. Remove excess clay.

6. Select a hexagon two sizes smaller for the inner opening. This will give you a 1.5mm hexagon frame.

7. With the whiteboard pen make a mark by the selected hexagon. Centre the geometric template over the clay. Use the needle tool upright to cut the inner edge. Keep the template in place as you lift the clay from the centre (the template will hold the clay in place and prevent distortion).

8. Place the hexagon so the tab is at the top. Use the oval cutter to make a lengthwise opening in the tab. Make sure it is equidistant from the sides of the tab and the inner edge. Cut any excess clay from the tab if needed.

9. Dry thoroughly, and then carefully refine the edges.

10. Fire for two minutes if the frame is small, or three minutes for a larger frame.

11. Wire brush as usual.

12. Place the hexagon on a steel block and tap gently all over with the nylon hammer to work-harden the frame.

13. Burnish and patina as desired.

14. Push open the oval jump ring. Insert the charm or decorative dangle and close the jump ring.

15. Push open the bail's ring and insert the frame (front first). Close the bail's ring.

CHAPTER THIRTEEN

Combination Pieces

BRINGING IT ALL TOGETHER! The projects covered previously can be assembled in different combinations to create a multitude of pieces and styles. In this chapter we will explore some of those combinations and design considerations.

MULTIPLE DISCS

A number of small discs arranged in a horizontal or vertical line creates beautiful pieces. Five discs slightly spaced out in the centre of a rolo chain make a pretty necklace. When the same five discs are attached in a straight line with a chain or connectors, they become a focal point. These combinations are easy to make, but must be planned carefully in order to correctly place the connecting openings.

FIVE DISC NECKLACE

You will need:
- Five x 8mm hammered discs (see Minimalist Pendant chapter).
- Five jump rings 3mm diameter, 22 gauge (0.64mm), to attach decorative elements.
- Two 3mm, 21 gauge (approximately 0.8mm) jump rings for clasp and end chain.
- Clasp and end chain.
- Chain, oval link or rolo link, 1.4mm x 41cm, either loose or ready-made.

1. Push open the 22 gauge jump rings.

2. Find the centre of the chain.

3. Insert one open jump ring into the central chain link. Add the disc, and carefully close the ring.

4. Equally space out the remaining four discs (two at either side) and attach in the same way. Make sure the chain is straight and that the links are in the same position. If not, the disc pendants will not hang properly.

RING AND LEAF PENDANT

A simple and elegant contemporary statement piece which can also be scaled down for a more subtle look. By combining different elements, the piece moves freely and draws attention.

The large jump rings echo the curves of the ring and the top of the leaf, making the design cohesive. The leaf has been narrowed to create the illusion of length and to economise on material.

You will need:
- 20mm (diameter) x 2mm (width) x 1mm (depth) seamless ring

(see Seamless Rings and Frames chapter).
• 35mm x 10mm leaf with a decorative element on the tip (see From Nature chapter). The bail hole should be large enough to accommodate an 8mm jump ring.
• Two 8mm diameter x 16 gauge open jump rings (1.3mm).
• Chain-nose pliers.
• Bent-nose pliers.
• Chain.

1. Push open the jump rings with the pliers.

2. Insert one jump ring through the hole in the leaf and then through the seamless ring.

3. Push close the jump ring.

4. Attach a second jump ring to seamless ring and then pass the chain through this jump ring.

Design options: The heavy gauge jump rings could be replaced by three light-gauge ones instead.

RING CLASP AND CHAIN PENDULUM

A simple way to add interest to a piece is to use the clasp as part of the design. In this project we will use a seamless ring attached to one end of the chain, and a disc at the other end. The disc acts as a stopper, securing the chain, but hangs loose and becomes a focal point.

You will need:
• 20mm x 1mm x 0.75mm seamless ring.
• 17mm disc.
• Two 3mm diameter, 21 gauge jump rings (approximately 0.8mm) to attach disc and ring.
• 60cm x 1.4mm loose chain, oval link or rolo link.
• Bent-nose pliers.
• Chain-nose pliers.

1. Slide open the jump rings with the pliers (hold the ring with bent-nose pliers and slide open with chain-nose pliers).

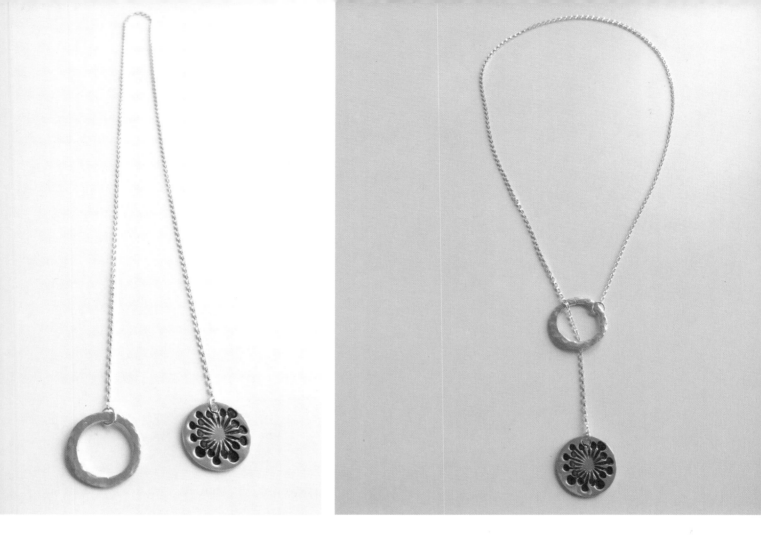

2. Pass one jump ring through the link at one end of the chain and then through the disc. Push close the jump ring.

3. Attach the second jump ring to seamless ring and then pass it through the link at the other end of the chain.

4. Push close the jump ring.

5. Gently feed the chain through the seamless ring to create a loop.

Please note the loop of chain should be long enough to go over the head.

Design options:
A. Instead of a disc use a coin pearl.
B. Multiple charms could be attached with a jump ring to the end of the chain.
C. Instead of a seamless ring, use a lobster clasp at one end of the chain, and attach a large pendant to the other. The lobster clasp can be hooked to any link, thus providing variety.
D. Layering different pieces in the same jump ring.

SMALL SEAMLESS RINGS AND PENDULUM EARRINGS

You will need:
- Two 3cm x 1mm/18 gauge sterling silver earring pendulums (see Versatile Rods chapter).
- Two 8mm diameter x 2mm x 1mm deep hammered seamless rings.
- Pliers: round concave pliers, chain-nose and flat-nose nylon jaw pliers.
- 3/4 hoop earrings.

1. Push open the small loops of the pendulums.

2. Insert the small loops into the small rings of the hoop earrings.

3. Close the small loops.

4. Push open the large loops of the pendulums.

5. Insert the small hammered seamless rings (textured end first).

6. Close the large loops.

CHAPTER FOURTEEN

Inspirational Gallery

A SHOWCASE OF METAL CLAY ADVANCED TECHNIQUES

'Adornment is a primitive desire. I love the idea of jewellery as a means of story-telling and self-expression. I'm intrigued by the idea of wearable art.'

Laragh McMonagle
Metal Clay Artist

Photography by Lisa Doyle: lisadoylephotography.co.uk, and by the author.

'Birdsong' Necklace and Sketchbook
Hand sculpted and dry construction.
Fine silver and freshwater pearls. 2014
Detail photo Lisa Doyle.
Sketchbook photo by the author.

'Baroque' Pendant
Carved. Rotating
central panel.
Fine silver, and
sterling beads. 2015
Photo Lisa Doyle.

'Floral Arrowhead'
Pendant
Hand embossed.
Fine silver. 2016
Photo Lisa Doyle.

'Tooth Fairy' Boxes
Hollow forming.
Fine silver. 2014
Photo Lisa Doyle.

**'Granulation' Pendant
and Chain**
Fine silver, and sterling
silver beads. 2018
Photo Lisa Doyle.

'Flora' Lapel Pin
Sculpted.
Fine and sterling
silver. 2015
Photo Lisa Doyle.

'Tribal' Ring
Mixed Media
Faux bone, fine silver
and sterling silver.
2010
Photo by the author.

'Moulin' Ring
Mixed Media
Copper, and fine
silver. 2010
Photo by the author.

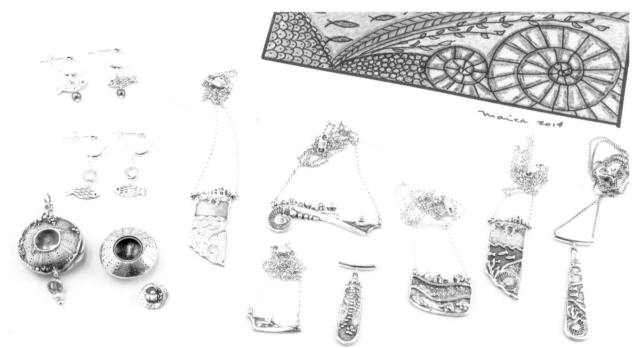

[**'Jurassic' Collection**
Hand embossed.
Fine silver and sterling silver. 2018
Photo by the author.

'Divine!' Perfume Bottle.
Hollow dry construction.
Fine silver, sterling chain, raw blue apatite crystal. 2017
Photo by the author.

'Sea Urchin' Locket
Hollow hand-sculpted.
Fine silver and freshwater pearl. 2005
Photo by the author.

Resources

SUPPLIERS

UK

www.thesilvercorporation.com
Silver findings, chain, wire, stringing materials, beads and tools.

www.cooksongold.com
PMC and Art Clay clays, findings, chain, wire and tools.

www.thepmcstudio.com
PMC clays, tools and accessories.

www.metalclay.co.uk
Art Clay clays, tools and accessories.

www.mailorder-beads.co.uk
Stringing materials, beads and tools.

www.palmermetals.co.uk
Metal clays, tools, jewellery findings, loose chain and stringing materials.

www.rayvenstudios.co.uk
Texture mats and Makers Mark Stamp.

USA

www.riogrande.com
Metal clays, jewellery findings, resins, and enamelling supplies.

www.cooltools.com
Clays, tools and equipment.

www.metalclays.com
Metal clays, tools, accessories and bespoke stamps.

AUSTRALIA
www.aussiemetalclay.com
Metal clays.

www.metalclay.com.au
Metal clays, tools and accessories.

NEW ZEALAND
www.beadaholic.co.nz
Silver clays, polymer clays and findings.

RUSSIA
www.metalclaystudio.ru
Specialist cutters, tools and texture mats.

BOOKS

Here are some of my favourites:

The Complete Metalsmith, Tim McCreight, (Brynmorgen Press Inc, 2004)

The Art of Jewellery Design: From Idea to Reality, Elizabeth Olver, (A & C Black Publishers Ltd, 2002)

Metal Clay Fusion, Gordon Uyehara, (Lark Crafts, 2012)

Metal Clay for Jewellery Makers, Sue Heaser, (Interweave Press LLC, 2012)

USEFUL WEBSITES

www.hallmarkingconvention.org
Information on international hallmarking laws.

www.esjd.co.uk
Metal clay, jewellery making and creative courses

www.metalclayacademy.com
Comprehensive information about metal clay.

Biography

MONICA WEBER-BUTLER has been a designer/maker/teacher for over twenty-five years. She enjoys creating contemporary narrative jewellery with silver and semi-precious stones, and immersing herself in the creative process, developing new techniques, and teaching her findings in both her studio in Beer and in Mexico. To this end, Monica established the Eclectic School of Jewellery and Design in December 2003. In Mexico she has taught several courses in a jewellery school and in an artist studio as a guest tutor.

'I aim to create designs which capture and celebrate nature by the inclusion of botanical details, graceful lines, delicate touches and a little whimsy. Traditional and modern techniques are used to add an extra dimension to my work and have become a signature on all of my jewellery pieces.'

Monica's jewellery has been exhibited in the UK and Mexico. Her work and articles have been featured in several UK magazines and in the Mexican Chamber of Jewellers' international magazine, the online magazine Metal Clay Today and in the PMC CONNECTION blog.

Monica was born in Mexico, but her heart made England her home in 1985. She studied Art and Design at the University of Westminster (London), and has an Honours Degree in Early Childhood Studies from the University of Plymouth and a City & Guilds Teaching Certificate. Early years teaching was initially her main focus, and she gained recognition in her field for quality and innovation in education. Having lived in London for fifteen years, she moved to the South West, to the charming village of Beer, where she has lived with her family since 2000. The Jurassic Coast, wildlife sightings, spectacular views and local landmarks have been a source of inspiration for her pieces. .

You can buy Monica's work in Coastal Craft Collective, Seaton, at Ilminster Arts Centre, or direct from her studio in Beer (by appointment), where she also teaches silversmithing, and a variety of creative subjects, including a weekly children's art class.

monicaweber.butler@me.com
www.esjd.co.uk